My Fishing Life

Wilburn E. Hall

All Rights Reserved
Copyright ©2015 Wilburn E. Hall
All photos, unless otherwise indicated, contributed by friends and members of the Hall family
Photo on page 98 reprinted with permission of *National Fisherman*
Produced by Teru Lundsten, Personal Historian
Book design and page layout by Tony Locke, Armchair ePublishing

Dedication

To my family, friends and fellow fishermen –
my life, as I remember it.

Contents

1. Early years — 7
2. First boats — 25
3. Joyce and the Mary Frances — 35
4. My brothers and shark fishing — 41
5. The Sea Breeze II — 49
6. The King and Winge — 55
7. The Rondys — 59
8. My hand — 61
9. More boats, more partners — 65
10. Family business — 77
11. Loss and joy — 83
12. Perfecting crab pots — 87
13. Crab peculiarities — 91
14. Fishing politics — 93
15. Celebrations — 99
16. Reflections — 103

Addenda:
Afterword, by Margaret Hall — 111
Chronology — 115
Maps — 118
Family — 120

Me as an infant with my mother, American Falls, Idaho

1. Early years

If I hadn't come up through the Depression, I'd have been a logging man like my dad. He was mostly a logger, but he did some farming too. His name was Evan Silas Hall. He originally came from Kentucky – born there in 1885.

Like a lot of families back there, they had lots of kids in their family, eleven of them. All the kids worked. They grew vegetables and tobacco. Dad later chewed a tobacco called Day's Worth and eventually his teeth wore out. He got false teeth but didn't quit chewing for a long time.

Dad's mother, Elizabeth Frasure Hall, was very well liked. She raised all the kids.

Grandfather Wilburn Hall, my dad's dad, was a "hard shell" Baptist. He didn't drink or smoke and always carried a Bible with him. Besides farming, he was also a "circuit rider," traveling around the country preaching.

Before he turned fifteen, Dad went up north to live with Uncle Evan Frasure in Ohio. Uncle Evan was a colonel in the Union Army during the Civil War. Dad was named after him and inherited his dark hair from the Frasures.

Dad came out to Oregon on a train in about 1901, with one of his brothers, perhaps John. They were both still teenagers. They spent a

Dad with his parents and siblings.
Seated, left to right: Mahala, his father Wilburn Hall, his mother Elizabeth Frasure Hall and John. Standing, left to right: Lee, Andy, Evan (Dad), Isabel and Bill.

My paternal grandparents Wilburn and Elizabeth Hall in their first garden in Sublet, Idaho, 1914.

My maternal grandfather, John Bernice Whisler, who served in the Civil War.

winter in Rainier, Oregon, logging fir timber using horses and bulls to skid the logs to where the flumes were. In the summer they went up to Walla Walla, Washington, to work in the wheat fields, then back down again to work in the woods near Rainier again. They stayed two years and then returned to Kentucky.

Idaho farm life

When Dad was a bit older, he and his younger brother Andy (we called him "Uncle Dock") went to Idaho to take advantage of the Homestead Act. Each person had to identify a section of 640 acres of undeveloped federal land, put a building on it and live on it for at least five years to qualify to keep it. Granddad and Grandmother Hall and others came soon after.

There were maybe ten families in the area where Dad was raised in Kentucky and all of them eventually moved to Sublet and American Falls, Idaho, and then on to Oregon and Washington. Dad and his family started in American Falls, but they were in the second wave of the Homestead Act and the only available land was on the upper ground that they couldn't irrigate. They had to dry farm and they didn't produce well. They could only get a crop every other year and consequently they'd have famines.

My mother, Ruth Ellen Whisler, was born in 1886 in Danville, Iowa. She caught scarlet fever and never really recovered. She and her three older sisters, Madge, Mayme and Maude, were all trained to be teachers in Mount Pleasant, Iowa, in what they called "normal school." After they went through high school they had to go for another year or two to earn their teaching credentials. That part was "normal school."

Their father, John B. Whisler, also took advantage of the Homestead Act and moved to Idaho with his wife, four daughters and son Everett. His wife died when Everett was born. Like Uncle Evan Frasure, Granddad Whisler also fought in the Civil War.

I'm not sure how they met, but my parents got married in 1916 and lived on my dad's homestead outside American Falls. Dad married late, relatively speaking, after he was thirty years old. Both my father and Uncle Dock needed to get married to get an increase in land, so that was another benefit of marriage. Dad continued to work with his

My mother, Ruth Ellen Whisler, before she married.

My Uncle Everett Whisler and his wife Sarah

brothers on their homesteads. They used horses to push combines in the fields.

My older brothers were born on September 20, 1917, there in American Falls on the farm. They were twins. Chester Lee was born first. Raymond's first name was John but they called him Ray.

I was born two years later, on August 9, 1919. I was named Wilburn Eugene Hall, after my father's father, Wilburn Hall. I don't know where "Eugene" came from.

We moved off the homestead when I was a couple of years old, because the homestead just didn't work out. Dad said they had a big hailstorm. It just flattened the wheat and ruined the whole crop. We moved to a log cabin on Uncle Everett Whisler and his wife Sarah's homestead outside Kendrick, Idaho, northeast of Lewiston, and lived there for about a year. Back then families really supported each other.

We then moved to a farm about three miles outside of Moscow. I remember them bringing in the hay in the summertime in Moscow, before my sister Frances was born. I remember when Frances was born, in October. I was about three years old. She was a blonde little baby – her hair was almost white.

We had a variety of animals on the farm, including Holstein cattle Dad got from the University of Idaho. They grazed on our farm through the winter, and then in the springtime Dad returned them to the university. We also had a shepherd dog named Jinx. He'd go bring in the cows. He was my favorite pet.

We also had a lot of chickens and a big ol' white rooster. He didn't seem to like me. He came running and jumped on my back and spurred me, scratching my back with his claws. He never bothered my brothers, just me.

Once Dad left his chewing tobacco out there in the barn and the three of us boys got it down to try. We took a little chew and we all ran to the horse trough outside where the water was to wash our mouths out. It didn't taste good at all – it burned.

After that we moved south to the Haga Ranch near the town of Kuna, Idaho. We lived there for a short time, maybe a year. Dad had a team of horses and helped different farmers put up hay.

They had a flume in one place that they used to bring water over for irrigation. (A flume is an open sloped chute whose walls are raised above the ground.) There were frogs in that flume and it froze up in winter. When the spring rains came the frogs thawed from the ice and they'd start coming to life. They'd been frozen solid in the ice, but by gory, they lived and came back to life.

Dad also had sheep on the ranch and the dogs ran in packs and kept you up at night attacking the sheep. One time a hawk was after a chicken and Mother used a revolver to shoot that hawk in one shot! Another time we boys were down the road and we killed a rattlesnake with a hoe.

When I was about six, I sat on the seat of the carriage. I said "Giddy-up!" to the horses and off they took. I didn't even have a-hold of the reins! Some fellow helped stop them after they took out a few mailboxes.

We had to haul water about a mile because there wasn't any water closer to the farm than that. We'd take the team of horses and big tanks and haul water home for drinking, washing dishes and bathing. Mother bathed us boys in a big washtub, one after the other.

We moved into the town of Meridian, about ten miles west of Boise. Back then Meridian was a tiny town with just one grain elevator and a creamery. I remember my parents had the paper delivered. Calvin Coolidge was President and I read about his big white collie living at the White House.

While we lived in Meridian, my dad went to see Great Uncle Lee, who had moved to Vernonia, Oregon. Our grandparents and Aunt Isabel and Uncle Ab Counts' family had moved there too. Dad wanted to see about getting work there because things had gotten pretty difficult in Idaho. It was 1924.

Dad got a job at the new lumber mill, the Oregon-American mill, the largest one in the world at the time. He was gone only a few weeks and came back to Idaho to get us: my mother, my brothers, Frances and me. Mary wasn't born yet. We moved to Vernonia to be closer to water, both rainfall and the ocean.

The forests of Vernonia

Dad had a Model-T truck. He fixed it up with sideboards and hard rubber tires. The tires weren't inflated like they are today, so it was a jolty ride to Vernonia.

On the way, in Pendleton, I saw Indians for the first time. By gory, their hair was braided and they dressed like natives in buckskin and feathers. We got through the Columbia River Gorge on a winding, narrow road through steep ravines. We arrived in Vernonia in the dark, and Uncle Lee was there to meet us.

Dad went to work at the lumber mill, hauling lath from the mill down to railroad cars. It was all old growth fir. They shipped the lath all over the nation, but mostly to the South and Midwestern states.

We boys enrolled at Corey Hill School that fall. They had "half grades." Chester was placed in a half grade behind Raymond because he had been sick in Idaho and missed a lot of school. I began first grade.

In Vernonia, money was pretty scarce, but about once a week Dad let us go to the movie theater. We saw some of the first cowboy shows with stars like Tom Mix or Rin Tin Tin, the dog.

Aunt Nan, Great Uncle Lee's wife, first took us to Sunday school at the Vernonia Christian Church. My Grandfather Hall held church in my grandparents' house. He continued traveling as a circuit rider preacher too. He traveled all over Oregon with Uncle Lee, meeting in peoples' homes. Once they were at a circus and saw some scantily clad women. Grandfather Hall said to Uncle Lee, "Let's get out of here *quick!*"

Left to right: Chester, grandmother Elizabeth, Uncle Ab (Absolum), Raymond, Frances, my father Evan and me in Vernonia, circa 1927

My father (on left) logging in Vernonia, 1929

Left to right: Me, Frances, Mary and Raymond when we visited Frances in Roseburg, Oregon, 1939

Mary, my youngest sister, was born in Vernonia in April of 1926. She had black hair when she was born, unlike Frances. After Mary was born my mother became ill, so I went to stay with Uncle Dock. He was portly but had a sunken chest. He wore pants with suspenders that were loose around the waist, but his pant legs were so tight, by gory, I wondered how he got his feet in them!

A year in Boise

That summer before school started, the summer of 1926, Uncle Lee took cousin Veda Drummond and me to the train station in Portland. Veda was moving from Vernonia back to Burley, Idaho, where her mother had already moved. Veda was one of the ladies who lost her husband in the flu epidemic during World War I.

In the late afternoon, Uncle Lee put us on a train that ran east. It was getting dark up the Columbia River Gorge and I slept only part time, waking up at every stop. We pulled into Boise the next day at noon and Dad's brother, Uncle Bill, was there to pick us up at the railroad station. He had a "Star Car," the one assembled by Durant Motors.

I stayed with Uncle Bill and Aunt Mildred that year for second

Left to right: Raymond, Mary, my father, Frances and me in Roseburg, Oregon, circa 1934

Left to right: Raymond, my father, me and Chester in Charleston, Oregon, 1938

Seated, left to right: Mary, Dad and Frances. Standing, left to right: Chester, me and Raymond

grade. On the way to school, I sometimes stopped at the Old Soldiers' home where Grandfather Whisler lived. He often had dribbles of poached egg in his whiskers. The home was only three blocks from Uncle Bill's on the west edge of town, and not far from Lowell Elementary School where I went to school. I saw a lot of other relatives in Boise too. I noticed that the Whisler side of the family gets gray hair or goes bald when the men get old. The Hall side often has really dark, thick hair.

    The next summer, in 1927, Uncle Bill took me back to Vernonia and when he returned to Boise, he took Frances with him. I think Aunt Mildred wanted a girl and I had been too much to handle for her. I was in too many fights.

    Back in Vernonia I lived with my Dad and my brothers again. My grandparents Hall still lived with Uncle Lee about two or three miles away. Mary lived with them too, because by then Mother was in the hospital in Salem.

There was a round cook stove in my grandparents' cabin and switches on the wall for punishing us grandkids. My grandparents slept in a very high bed and Grandma stored big squashes under it. She had a square bedside table, oak I think, with ornate edging carved around it, all covered with medicine bottles, dozens of them! She wore lots of dirndl dresses and skirts with petticoats that came down nearly to her ankles.

The coast: Waldport

We moved to Waldport just after New Year's 1930, when school was out for the Christmas holidays.

I came from Vernonia with my father driving the truck. We got loaded up and, by gory, we had that truck piled full! In those days they canned a lot of food and we had fruit jars galore. It was snowing as we drove over Alsea Mountain.

The rest of them came in a car down by a different route, through Willamina, to the ferry at Waldport. In the car with Chester and Ray were the housekeeper, Martha, and her little girl named Bessie, who was about three years old. Dad had hired Martha to cook and clean house since Mother was in the hospital. Frances and Mary weren't with us because by then they were living with other relatives.

We all arrived the same day. It had snowed all night and there was probably fourteen inches of snow on the ground.

When we first arrived in Waldport my dad became a partner in an alder mill, which they converted from a salmon cannery. It was about a mile up the Alsea River at the edge of town. There were more alder trees along the coast than there were inland so they had high hopes. So after a while we moved to Drift Creek, on the north side and inland of the river.

Once, in Drift Creek, I got poison oak. Man alive, did that itch! To relieve it we used blue vitriol, which stung. Another time Chet rode down to Charleston and back on a horse. I put on his pants later and after a while they started itching because Chet had ridden through a poison oak patch. That time I had to get a shot to take care of it.

I was one of fourteen kids in the school in Drift Creek with a teacher who graduated from Stanford University. This was only for the first part of the sixth grade because we moved back to Waldport, into a house near the school that winter. This is about the time both Raymond and Chester went back to Vernonia.

Raymond returned to Vernonia to stay with Grandpa Hall after Grandma died in 1932, because Uncle Lee had gotten married to Aunt Mildred and moved with Mary to a new house. Then Raymond moved to Boise where he was a star wrestler and finished school there. He attended business school for three months before returning to Waldport.

Even though he's older than I am, Chester was placed in my class at Waldport School because he'd missed more school and they didn't have half-grades like in Vernonia. He also moved back to Vernonia for a while, then to Boise for a couple of years, then finally back to Waldport for his senior year to graduate with me.

I was separated a lot from my siblings when I was growing up, especially from my sisters after my mother got sick. My dad was busy working and I guess he couldn't handle five kids by himself. But the family communicated by postcards. My dad had a trunk that was a third full of postcards. But my brothers and I always stayed in touch with our sisters throughout our lives and have visited whenever we could.

My Uncle Bill kept Frances. She went to school in Boise and graduated there, and eventually became a registered nurse. Frances married Duff Leaver and started her family in Birmingham, Alabama, and later they moved to North Carolina.

Uncle Lee raised Mary in Vernonia. She called him "Daddy Lee" and our dad "Daddy Evan." My brothers and I paid for her college in Fairbanks, Alaska. Mary married Jim Binkley and raised a family in Fairbanks.

* * *

When there was just the two of us in Waldport, Dad and I moved into an army tent with a cook stove. I was about fourteen. Sometimes I was left to fend for myself while my dad was logging. Neighbors looked in on me so I got by. I had nothing but a sack of oatmeal to eat – well, eggs and farina too. By gory, to this day, I still love oatmeal.

When we first got to Waldport, the ferry to cross the Alsea Bay was just a barge that held six cars. About 1934 they built a bridge at Waldport, the Alsea Bay Bridge. It sure saved a lot of time.

My mother died that same year, in 1934, four years after we moved to Waldport. She had spent some of this time with Aunt Madge and Uncle Weidel in Idaho, but they couldn't manage her, so she was sent to a hospital in Pendleton. I was fifteen when she died.

When I was about sixteen, I built a float house for Dad and me to live in. I towed down some logs from up the river and sawed grooves in them. It worked pretty well. Chester returned and lived with us too. I kept track of the costs and sold the float house the next year for just a little profit.

Growing up in Waldport, my best friend was a boy named Arleon Parsons. Arleon and I were together a lot. With my dad gone so much, Arleon's dad, Bill Parsons, had a big effect on my life. He was the Sunday school teacher and very religious. He built my faith. He told us lots of Bible stories, about the prophets and divine revelation. I was "sprinkled" (that's a form of baptism, as opposed to pouring or immersion) as a Presbyterian when I was a sophomore, along with other classmates.

At various times Mr. Parsons was also the postmaster, the grade school principal, and my eighth grade teacher. Every time a kid misbehaved in class, Mr. Parsons put an X on the blackboard. Once you had four Xs he took you to the woodshed and paddled your rump. I never let it happen to me, though. Discipline like that was good for kids. All the kids respected him. They thought he was fair and honest. Like they say, "Spare the rod, spoil the child."

My sixth grade class at Waldport School, 1931. I am in the first row, third from left. My brother Chester is hiding behind the flowers. My friend Arleon Parsons is in front of the flowers

My class at Waldport High School. Chester is on the far left of the second row. I am in the center of the back row

Me at 17½

What a Team, 1937. A cartoon by my classmate at Waldport High, Naomi Wolfe (I was known to blush)

The Tupper *(or* Sea Falcon*) in the fog*

2. First boats

Lure of the sea

The first time I saw the ocean was over the July 4 weekend when we lived in Vernonia. We went up to Astoria, through it to the seaside and down the coast near Wheeler. We spent one or two nights there. We had mattresses with us to sleep on at night, near the car.

The first boat I had any experience on was at Waldport, on Alsea Bay. I was about twelve, I guess. Dad got a rowboat and two sets of oars. It was a cedar boat, like a dory, about sixteen feet long. It was really light, but it had quite a bit of beam so it was pretty stable.

Dad later used it for crabbing with crab rings in the bay. We'd dig shrimp for bait and catch some perch. We'd go clamming too, for razor clams. It sure kept us busy! At first Dad dug all the clams but finally he got more shovels and we joined in. We could see clams better than Dad could because we were less tall and we were closer to the ground, plus our eyesight was better. We could see their imprint in the sand – it was kind of like a doughnut. They'd spew up and taper off so there was a round hole and the sand around it would be wet. Sometimes you'd hit the ground and the clam would pull its neck down in the little hole, maybe 3/8 to a half inch across, and suck you down when you were trying to get it. Later on when we got better we'd dig out in the surf. The Hunter brothers and the Reinertsen and Greshaber kids went clamming too.

Another boat Dad bought was even smaller. It was a round-bottomed boat made of galvanized metal with rivets every few inches over the lap. It was a lifeboat originally, owned by some big ship. I don't think it even had a name. It had a four horsepower gas Regal engine, and I learned to run it. I used it to tow logs that had fallen into the slough. I went about a half mile to the trestle, around the point to the mill. Two guys said they'd pay me for them, but they didn't. They were crooked as a dog's back leg, so I quit.

The first time I saw a real fishing operation I went out with a fellow named Charlie Hunter, one of the three Hunter brothers. The other two were Harold and W.S. W.S. helped run the plant in Waldport. Charlie had a boat named *Bubbles* that he bought in Seattle, a trawler that caught salmon out in the ocean. He bought a half dozen crab pots too. I went out with him as a helper, crabbing in five or six fathoms along the shore.

One time I went out with him and he ran out on about a half-full tide and pulled the pots and they were chock full of crabs. He had to run back in on high water because the bar was so shallow where the Alsea River flows out to sea.

I didn't do any work, I just watched him. I was probably in about sixth or seventh grade. I thought it was interesting. I saw that he did well, but that it took a lot of skill.

Later on in Waldport, we tried to sell fish for crab bait to fishermen, perch that we'd catch around the pilings. Forked tail perch were about twelve to eighteen inches long. They were rainbow colored and had a V-shaped tail. We called them squawfish.

We figured out that perch like barnacles. The perch hit the pilings and knocked the barnacles loose. They'd suck out the gelatin from inside the barnacles and spit it out. We'd take the barnacles and put a hook through them, let it drift down and see the perch come up, jerk the pole and hook them. We'd get maybe fifty pounds of them to sell for about a dollar for crab bait.

We used to go out at night and fish too, for an hour or two. We'd go out about half tide to low water. Mud flats crossed to the north side of Alsea Bay, and flounder went up on high tide and then drifted back with the tide. We'd hang a lantern out over the bow and see flounder, flatfish with both eyes on one side of their heads, quivering their fins.

We'd put water in a live box in the boat, about six to eight inches deep, and spear the flounder with a three-tined pitchfork. They'd stay alive in the box in the boat. We'd filet them out and sell them to a few restaurants in town.

Money was scarce but we didn't realize how in debt the economy was. We were too young to understand, and we always had enough. We had milk all the time from different farmers or the creamery in Waldport. We planted a garden and raised all our potatoes and fresh vegetables, some for canning. We hunted for deer and canned that too. If we needed a bit more money we'd go cut brush and Dad cleared land. We had enough money to pay a lady named Mrs. Taylor to wash and iron my shirts.

The fall of '36, all up and down the coast there were lots of fires because it was extremely dry. They brought in men from Portland to fight fires. Some of them were winos – they picked them up on the waterfront up there, I guess to keep them off the streets. They weren't very ambitious. They also brought in Negroes from back east, and conscientious objectors. We called them "Concies." They stayed down at Camp Angel south of Waldport.

Fellows from the "3-C" camps, the Civilian Conservation Corps, also fought the fires. They came from all over the United States – a lot of them came west to build trails and roads and campsites. The 3-C guys got a dollar a day and their room and board for fighting the fires.

The forest rangers came to the school to recruit juniors and seniors to fight fires too. You didn't have to go, but if you did they'd take you out on the fire line. Most of the time it was Friday, Saturday and Sunday and you'd go to school the other four days of the week. I think once or twice they took us out to build trails, but mostly it was to fight fires. It was my senior year. I got to supervise a high school group, to keep track of them, and I earned three dollars a day on the fire line.

We'd have to move the vegetation out and make a trail about three feet wide. We'd cut the wood with an ax so the fire crossed underneath and we built a trail around the edges of the fire. Sometimes they'd start a backfire to meet the other fire, if the wind was blowing in the right direction so that you could do it safely. That way you'd prevent the fire from jumping across the high trees.

We fought fires until Thanksgiving Day, when they brought us turkey sandwiches. It started to drizzle, and that was the end of firefighting.

When we weren't at school, we went out fishing on Alsea Bay or a bit south off Cape Perpetua, and sold the crabs we caught. Alsea Bay has quite a bit of fresh water from rains, especially in the winter. Crabs won't live in fresh water, but fresh water rises to the top, above the salt water underneath. The crabs could feed on the bottom, in the salt water.

We'd keep live boxes, fairly deep ones, maybe five to seven feet deep, and we used to have retail stands along the coast to sell to the tourists. We were able to earn more money fishing than we did fighting fires or logging. Logging, we just got $2.50 a day.

Dad was logging at Cape Arago near Charleston and got me a job with the Counts, Aunt Isabel's sons, who were cutting timber one summer. I worked there until school started again. I also worked with lumber, on the grounds, not in the mill itself.

We also worked for Pacific White Cedar Corporation, out of Coos Bay. We felled fir trees and bucked them up for the mill that was going to cut them into railroad ties.

Dad was very particular about telling me about safety, on the first job I had bucking logs. Caterpillar came out with a new set of blades and pulleys to flatten roads for logging roads. I worked in the right-of-way and had to watch out for them.

What it came down to was, you either worked in the logging industry or you fished in the bay. You could make a livelihood either way, but fishing was better money. Guys were getting hurt once in a while in the woods. That helped me choose too.

I broke into fishing on other boats, crabbing in five or six fathoms. They didn't want to hire me, because I was a greenhorn, but I first went out when I was between my junior and senior year, down at Coos Bay because Dad was logging near there.

The *Tupper*

When I was a sophomore they elected me treasurer of the high school. The only income we had was from basketball and football games. It wasn't much.

I had no idea how to manage money, so the principal explained to me, "You've got two columns. One is for the money that comes in. The other is for the money that goes out. You subtract what goes out from what comes in. You can't send out more than what you bring in." From that I thought, "Gee, I better take some classes here."

Some girls in my school were preparing for secretarial work. They were taking typing and I took it too. I was the only boy in the class. I got up to 53 words per minute the first year but couldn't get past that. I didn't gain speed because I think the muscles in my fingers from heavy work didn't help.

I took bookkeeping too. The athletic teams were like businesses to run – you had to maintain inventory and order equipment. Both bookkeeping and typing helped out later in my businesses. I could type out a business letter, write it out first and then type it. Later on when I lost my hand my wife Joyce did the typing.

During the fall of my senior year, a fellow with the last name Leeper hired Chet and me to start knitting crab pots, putting the webbing on the frames. He also taught us how to hang tunnels. We'd work after school until dark. That kept us busy and helped out financially.

My brothers and I bought the *Tupper* around the first of the year, my last year of high school. I suppose it was about January, in 1937. We heard about a boat for sale down in Coos Bay, and went down and looked at it. The owner told us he got seasick and that's why he wanted to sell the boat. We had about $600, saved up from crab fishing and fighting fires, and so we gave $400 down. I wrote a contract out for $2,600: $400 down, and we paid 25% of the gross catch to him every month, no interest.

We didn't know about taxes and didn't pay any at first. After about two years, Aunt Madge's husband Weidel Kjossness got us to thinking about it, so we got a guy named Joe Wilson to fill out our first tax form.

The *Tupper* was a nickname; the *Sea Falcon* was the real name. The guy that built it was named Tupper. It was a clean V-style boat, 38 feet long. It was built really strong, solid framed with Port Orford cedar frames and planking outside with fir decking.

Dad and Raymond fished it with crab rings. For bait they used pilchards, a kind of herring, or razor clams (even though they were illegal), or else barnacles they scraped off the ferry pier. In May, Chet and I graduated from high school. One night they gave out diplomas and the next day we were all loaded up and drove to Coos Bay in Dad's Model A Ford.

Dad didn't like to fish. He was afraid that the anchor wouldn't hold. We stayed out overnight and he couldn't sleep, he was so worried. Plus, we began to learn that things on the boat weren't in the best condition and that boats had to be maintained.

Baiting was different back in the '30s. Women sewed cotton bait bags dipped in bluestone copper, which was dissolved in water, and then treated the bags with wax. The hot wax dripped in between the fibers and it made the bags stiff so they wouldn't rot as quickly, and it killed all the germs too – the copper kept the microbes out. It's what we used for bait boxes before plastic came in. I still remember one of the women who did that, Mrs. Berglund.

Sometimes they dipped the bags in tar, but the bags couldn't be used right away because they had to seal. They gradually leaked a little bit of oil out of the tar – that's how they sealed. It took awhile. We'd hang them down in the water and let them wash for a couple of weeks before we started baiting them.

Usually the bait is frozen when you get it, maybe the night before for the next day. We usually used herring, sometimes cod heads. We chopped our own bait in chunks with a heavy blade, like a cleaver, big and heavy with a steel handle. Eventually they developed baiting machines with electric motors, and then hydraulic motors, to rotate the blades.

We put forty- to fifty-pound packages in a freezer and wiggled off quarter-foot chunks as we needed them. They broke off easily. We'd put the chunks of bait in a barrel and mount the barrel on the bulkhead or the bow so that it was out of the way and off the deck.

When we were hanging bait, we hung each piece of bait on a great big safety pin and dropped it down into the water with a spring on it and it stayed there. We put it in the pot and pulled it through a mesh on top with a lid on it. We pulled it down below the entryway. Fresh bait made the fishing go faster. Small crabs escaped and if the rest were pulled in tight you didn't have much measuring of crab to do. We grabbed the crab with our left hands and our right hands measured its size.

By the end of a trip the leftover bait broke down and the odor got down to the bait boxes or bait bags. It smelled like fish, but after the trip we'd wash them all up.

In the *Tupper*, we fished in outside waters. We didn't fish in the bay. They had small boats that fished in the bay. We'd go north of them toward the Umpqua River, nineteen miles from the buoy whistler. We used davits to pull the lines in. We'd throw the line up to the buoy and then pull down on the gurdy.

Because the *Tupper* was built for outside waters, we had a larger boat than the bay crabbers had at Coos Bay or Waldport. Most of those boats were 25 to 35 feet long and they were double-enders. The *Tupper* had a round stern and a higher bow and really was pretty seaworthy for the size of it, 38 feet. It had a thirty horsepower hand crank Fairbanks Morris diesel engine in it. It had a lever on top of the cylinders that pulled the exhaust from one of the valves down and you could spin it to start it. It had a heavy flywheel you'd lift so the valves would cut in and they'd fire right off the first try.

At Yaquina Bay, you wanted to get back to port on high water over the bar if there were any swells to get in. You wanted to ride the waves in. It was a big concern, but it wasn't as big as it was for some of the other boats that were coming down from the north. There were several boats that were much larger.

There were big tides in Yaquina Bay. In minus tide you'd run pretty hard, maybe ten feet over the bar, and if you happened against a swell you'd get really wet. It was easier and safer to get over the bar on high water.

For a long time they didn't do a good job of maintaining the depth at Yaquina Bay. They lost so many boats coming up the inside, sailboats especially, depending on the wind. The entrance to the bay was wide and shallow up the inside, and you could see the reef underwater even in heavy swells. It wasn't until after World War I that men in diving suits blasted out the reef. Now that they have dredged it, the water is about forty feet deep.

We fished marine crabs for a while then in summertime we moved up to Winchester Bay. We fished from the Umpqua north to

Heceta Head. Sometimes we'd be the only ones who had pots there.

Different fisheries roll in cycles, so we'd go to some other type of fishery to fill in the year. At first we fished for crab year-round, but then we started fishing for albacore tuna in the summer too, alternating with crabs, and silver salmon in the fall. It varied different years.

We started trucking our crabs to Coos Bay. One time we drove there in an old Model A Ford through Riverton and Bandon, through a flood. At that time there wasn't a road down from Charleston down along the coast, so you had to go through Coquille. There was a low area in the road and we went though the water loaded down with about a ton of window weights that we used to make the crab pots heavier. The fenders were almost down on the tires, by gory! We didn't know if we'd make it, but we did.

Then one of Harold Hunter's sons started a crab plant in Waldport. We trucked our crabs there because there were so many fishermen down in Coos Bay you couldn't sell many crabs. We had pickups and put trailers on them.

Then we bought a ton-and-a-half Chevrolet truck with a flatbed that we could load our boxes on and haul about 120 dozen crabs, about a boatload. Later on we built the plant at Newport and moved up here after four years fishing down there.

When we unloaded the boats early on, on the *Tupper*, we didn't have good lights or generators so we'd plug in a little dim light. Sometimes it was totally dark. We grabbed the crabs and threw them in the plant's boxes quickly before they could pinch you.

At the plant in Newport, women processed the crabs after we delivered them. Depending how many they had to process, the number of workers ranged from six to fifteen women. When they worked, they wrapped their hair in full head bandanas, and were as poor as Job's turkeys. They were paid to pick out the meat by the pound, maybe 300-500 pounds per day. They weren't paid much and they only worked five or six hours a day.

First the crabs were sorted into dozens, in three grades: small, medium and large. The women used hammers to crack the crab shells and shake out the meat. Then the crabmeat was vacuum-packed into small six-ounce tins or large five-pound tins.

When we delivered crab directly to retail stands, we learned the hard way not to let them have more than five dozen crabs without paying us for them up front.

Eventually we sold the *Tupper* to a couple of our crewmen, Kenny Dodd and Gus Wagner. It was sold several times after that, and eventually abandoned on a beach. The port authorities burned it about ten years ago.

June 15, 1941

3. Joyce and the Mary Frances

In 1940 we had the *Mary Frances* built at Charleston, Oregon, down toward the mouth of Coos Bay. An older fellow, Mr. Green, and a young assistant built it. It took about six months to build. We named the boat after our two sisters.

Joyce and I met in Winchester Bay, where she lived. We met at someone's birthday party. The boys and I were fishing out of there and sometimes we played tennis in town in the evenings. Joyce's stepfather was working timber and then he began having heart problems and so they filed saws for other companies. In the summer they smoked salmon for people.

Joyce was a good-looking gal. Like most girls, she took home economics. She became a good cook and seamstress – she was very adept with the whole thing.

She was a senior in high school when we began going together. We went together for a while, and then I got her an engagement ring. That was before the first of the year, 1941. We set the wedding date for June 15, after she graduated. We were married in Winchester Bay and honeymooned at Yosemite National Park. At the end of that summer we moved to Newport and rented a house close to Nye Beach. It was across the street from the Christian church that I still attend.

With Joyce, summer 1940

Then we bought our house on Abbey Street, in Newport, in 1942, in the fall of the year, after Bonnie was born. We bought it from Claire and Victor Bump. It was originally built for Claire's mother. They had ordered it from Georgia Pacific, which constructed it in sections at the lumber mill in Toledo and put it together in Newport. It set on a good foundation because they used a lot of cement and good rocks.

I told Joyce, "This would be a good house because we could see the bar." It had two large picture windows facing the ocean. It set high on a knoll a block west of Highway 101. Abbey Street came over the knoll and dead-ended. The other end led to the waterfront. The Abbey Hotel was nearby. It was the biggest hotel in town and people used to come in on the railroad and they'd go to the beach. Some rented little summer cabins near the beach.

I used a room built under the garage for storing nets and other gear. It was accessible through a trap door in the garage and by a wooden door in the basement. It sure smelled like fishing gear in a concentrated space! Vic Bump owned a machine shop down on the waterfront and later I stored and worked on my gear on the upper floor of his shop. I hung buoys on the rafters.

Joyce understood the fishing regulations, and she'd sign for things and make out the checks. She did all the bookkeeping because I was busy fishing on the *Mary Frances* with my brothers, who had moved up here too. We were all delivering to the Newport plant by then.

Eventually Joyce and I had the rest of our kids. She had quite a bit of labor problems with Bonnie, our firstborn, but after that it was easier. At least her mother was up here when Bonnie was born, in April of '42. The doctors had a large home they turned into a maternity hospital. Janet was born there, and then Vern was born there too. Margaret was born over in Toledo, in Lincoln Hospital, Lincoln County, on Lincoln's birthday. I told her later on that we would have called her Abe after Lincoln if she had been a boy. It's always been a family joke.

No doubt being away a lot strains your relationships with your kids. I had an offer to go down south and fish tuna, but I'd have been gone for a month or two at a time, so I passed it up. Some guys in San Francisco heard about my fishing record, and they offered to bring me

Me hanging diapers to dry, "Dad's Duty"

in as skipper on the big tuna boats, but I turned them down. Margaret, our youngest, was in high school before I went to Alaska.

I never stayed out crab fishing for long. I'd be a couple days home and one night out. We'd get in sometimes at midnight, but we'd just stay on the go because usually they wanted to start processing the crab in the plant right away. But at least we were near home.

We lost the *Mary Frances* in '43, about a year after we moved to Newport. The engine in it was built in Oakland, California. Turns out it had a bad transmission. When it stopped the outside gear revolving, in neutral, it would go into reverse. It wasn't a real good gear.

It broke right out here on the Newport Bar. It was foggy when they were coming in, and there was no radar in those days. I wasn't on the boat; Jack Hawley was running it. It got around the north jetty when the transmission broke and the guys jumped off. One guy got hurt a little because he skidded on the rocks. Otherwise there were no major injuries, but we lost the boat.

Someone said he'd get some sticks of dynamite and blow that rock out and then they'd pull the boat back. Well, the dynamite blew the whole stern of the boat off and never moved the rock. The keel and propeller went down deeper, behind the rock. The boat was a complete loss. It got beat up when the surf picked up. We had it insured, at least, for $4,500, about what we paid for it.

The Mary Frances

The Christian *on Lake Washington*

4. My brothers and shark fishing

The *Ruth Ellen* and the *Sunset*

My brothers and I had the *Ruth Ellen* built at Coos Bay, in 1943. We named it after our mother. Back then the town was called Marshfield. Years later they combined North Bend and Marshfield into one common name, Coos Bay.

A Scandinavian built it, Abe Elfving. It was well built. It was a 53-foot boat, larger than the *Tupper*. Five or six men worked for Abe, all Scandinavians too. They all worked on it. I think at that time they were getting $1.50 an hour. The whistle blew and they were all there and ready at eight o'clock in the morning. They didn't have a coffee time back then, they just carried a mug around and set it down here and there and once in awhile went over and got a gulp while they were working. They didn't get coffee breaks until the unions came.

About the same time we saw the *Sunset* at Charleston. It was a "smoker" because the Fairbanks Morse diesel engine put out a lot of smoke. It was up for sale. The New England Fish Company owned it and we bought it from them. It used to tie up at Empire, up the bay about three or four miles from Charleston. Chester went to school for a year, at Northwest Bible College in Seattle (now it's in Kirkland), before we bought the *Sunset*.

Most of the time on the small boats we had just two guys. Once in a while we'd take an extra to wash buoys. At the most there were three of us: the skipper and two crewmen. Usually Ray skippered the *Ruth Ellen*, Chester the *Sunset*, and I ran the *Christian*.

The *Christian*

In 1944 we built the *Christian* at a boatyard in Kirkland, Washington, on Lake Washington, and brought it down to Newport during the Christmas season, right after the first of the year, in early 1945.

We stayed in Seattle while it was being built and had to take a ferry from Madison Street diagonally across Lake Washington, northeast to Kirkland. I'd be in the pilothouse up high in the middle of the ferry. The air would get cool and the water would be warm, so it got foggy. They had a bell at the terminals, like a church bell, and they'd ring that thing in the fog, even in the wee hours, so the ferry could steer toward it. They didn't have any radar back then on the ferry. Sometimes you couldn't see over 150 feet ahead of you. It didn't haul too many cars. Later on you could drive around Lake Washington. It was probably 25 miles to drive around, but it was only a couple of miles across the water.

My brothers and I didn't serve in World War II because we got occupational deferments. The military called us up to Portland with a group of other fishermen, like Larry Cooper, and asked us to bring our fish tickets as evidence of our occupation. Since we fished year-round and produced food year-round, we were deferred. But the trollers like Larry were drafted because they tied their boats up by the middle of October. Salmon season was over by then and they wouldn't start fishing again until the next spring. I also got married in June of 1941, before the war started in December, so that was another reason to give me a deferment.

Plus they needed shark livers for the British and American air forces. They said vitamin A improved night vision that aided bombing Germany. We caught sharks later in the war for their livers, so we were contributing to the war effort that way. One time we set a record of 10,000 pounds of shark livers in one delivery.

We had about 2½ miles of nets that were 90-mesh deep with a

10½-inch mesh. The mesh was diamond shaped. The sharks ran their noses through it and as they got back by their gills it compressed. Sharks have sandpaper skin, so they'd roll up in the net.

I put refrigeration on the *Christian* to haul shark livers during the war until they got synthetic vitamins. By the end of the war, pharmaceutical companies began to make vitamin A, but they were never sure if it was as good as the natural oils from shark livers. Still, the shark fishery went downhill as soon as the synthetic vitamin A came in.

When we quit shark fishing, we gave the nets to pea farmers, just to get rid of them. Shark nets can support quite a lot of pea vines.

While we were fishing on the *Christian* during the war, my dad worked logging in northern California. He met a woman named Margaret and married her. Then he worked at Kaiser Shipyard in Richmond, California, so my dad helped the war effort too.

Adventures on the *Christian*

Once we were shark fishing off California, and the weather was pretty flat so I was taking an afternoon snooze on the bunk before we'd lay the nets out at night. We had a crewman who was part Indian, and he was napping too. I woke up, but he was still sleeping soundly, so we warmed up a bottle of mercurochrome, pulled his T-shirt up and painted his stomach red. He didn't notice it for a day or so. When we finally mentioned it to him, he was good-natured about it. The cook said, "Well, you're part redskin so we anointed you red."

My most thrilling experience at sea was probably cutting a net off a whale off of California. We saw a whale floating on the surface, all tangled up in a little chain and ropes and nets. He was just as thin as could be – we could see his backbone. We were on the *Christian* and he lay alongside of us and he didn't try to swim away.

He just let us work. We had a hook with a four-foot bite in it with a sharp point so we could reach down underneath and cut all that chain and net and rope off him and set him free. Then he went off. I don't know if he survived or not. Never will know but it was something you don't forget.

Another time we were on the *Christian* and it was blowing about a hundred miles an hour. The wind lifted roofs here in town, blew in windows, blew trees over. We were coming in and came up to the bar.

On the Christian *with Chester (on right)*

Waves were breaking over the bar. We were out near the whistler buoy offshore. They just had a can, with no bell hanging on it.

We were about even with the buoy and looking at the bar and it wasn't looking good. By then it was blowing a gale. I stood on top of the pilothouse in a life preserver. It was spraying, so I put the boat in reverse and we came parallel with the swell but we couldn't pull the boat back through. The propeller lifted in the air above the water, so we couldn't pull her over the backside. The waves took us in about a few hundred yards and we broached. Another hundred yards and we would have stood up straight, stern up in the air.

But as it was, the boat lay on its side, but it didn't capsize because it was heavy. It had about three tons of galvanized clinker washers back there between the fuel tanks in the bottom of the boat.

The engine had a safety feature to prevent it from overheating. If the water got too hot or if the oil pressure dropped, it would cut the engine off. The engine had a lever on it that we'd pull up to start the engine again, but if you lost the lever, then you couldn't start it again – no fuel went to the engine. We went in on a breaker and we broached around sideways, and the boat took quite a bashing. By that time we were in about eight fathoms of water so we were looking at a breaker about forty feet high.

We were outside the north jetty and the engine died. I knew immediately so I sent Jack Hawley down and said, "Pull that lever out and start the engine!" He ran right down and tried but no pressure was coming. The boat turned around, its bow pointing out to sea. By the time we finally started the engine there was another set of breakers coming but they weren't as big as the others, so we made it through them. We went back out and then came back in the next day.

The force of the water hitting the wheelhouse pulled all the nails out of all the trim. But it didn't knock any windows out. That was one of those scary times. I thanked the Lord that we made it.

After that I designed a hook to prevent the engine from dying. Anytime you'd cross the bar or have any other trouble you'd get that hook in the lever so it wouldn't turn the fuel off. The hook had an eye in it. I hooked the lever up on a pipe so it'd hold it up while you were in dangerous waters.

This safety feature controlled the oil pressure and the heat of the engine so you wouldn't ruin your engine if it got hot. Later on they put temperature gauges up in the pilothouse with bells on them – an alarm system. But we didn't have one back then.

Partners no more

My partnership with my brothers broke up in 1948. Chester was a really good conversationalist, better than Raymond or me. Chester was a good fisherman but when he got on shore, he liked to talk. He would have made a better preacher. When he got onshore he never worked much, getting gear ready or anything else, so we'd send him back on the boat fishing. He did a little more then, but Raymond and I thought he didn't work his fair share.

We decided to break up. We owed more money on the *Christian*, but the *Ruth Ellen* was practically paid for, and we had paid for the *Sunset*. Chester had taken a year off and it was Raymond's turn to go to school. He went to business school in Boise for three months, but then he dropped out.

After our partnership broke up, we each took the boats we had run before. Chester took the *Sunset* and I took the *Christian*. Eventually, after he was out of school, Raymond took the *Ruth Ellen*.

The *Sunset* was still fishing a few years ago. It was at Crescent City or somewhere down there in California. I don't know where it is now. The *Ruth Ellen*, I don't know what happened to it either. The *Christian* ran for years in southeast Alaska. It tendered salmon and ran supplies to small communities on islands. It may still be working, for all I know.

The Sea Breeze II

5. The Sea Breeze II

In 1949 I sold the *Christian* and bought the *Sea Breeze II*. I sold the *Christian* to Parks Canning Company in Alaska and they hauled salmon with it. Last I heard it's still hauling salmon around Puget Sound, and goes north during salmon season to Ketchikan, Alaska.

I bought the Sea Breeze II from a Finn named Uno Pykonen. They used to say when they introduced us, "Do you know Pykonen here?" It was a pun on his first name ("you know" rhymes with "Uno"). Uno lived here in Newport and got it built up at Lincoln City on the Siletz River where it runs by Taft and then into the ocean. It was built about a mile or two up the river from the ocean.

The Sea Breeze II was a smaller boat. It was 52 feet long, and had a Cummins engine and a good reverse gear in it. The Christian was 70 feet long, but a 52-foot boat was more maneuverable for crab fishing. You run more gear with it and it turned more sharply. We could average fifty pots an hour.

Right after the war the U.S. built fifty boats in Bath, Maine that were given to European countries because their fleets were wiped out by the Germans, so they didn't have food. They built these boats to help the Europeans get back into production.

At the time, in Europe, they didn't have refrigeration plants to hold the food. People who had the money got refrigeration right away, but people who didn't had to wait until the U.S. lent them money to build fish plants and refrigeration so they could freeze the product. The

U.S. put a lot of money into this.

Then the world market started to change. Europeans shipped fish into the U.S. and they put laws in their countries that said you couldn't ship fish into their countries, so our fish markets went down because of that. Norway, Sweden – all of them began to build boats and produce out in the North Sea. They'd fish and ship their catch to the U.S., and they could get a better price. It hurt us because we couldn't compete with them. It took years to recover from that.

When I fished down off Coos Bay, the price of crab was about 10¢ a pound, but sometimes I got more because I bargained. Once I unloaded and asked the fish man for 14¢ a pound. He came up to 12¢ from 10¢. One time we unloaded about 30,000 pounds with a deck load at Crescent City because we got a good price. It brought the price up to 12¢ in both Coos Bay and Newport.

Once on the *Sea Breeze II*, we were after albacore way offshore and we saw a pod of whales spouting. Usually it's a sign of fish – when they are spouting they are feeding on some kind of fish. If we lucked out it was albacore, so we'd approach the whales and test the water around them for fish.

We approached the pod of whales and saw that killer whales were trying to get a baby whale in the pod, a different kind of whale than than an orca, cradled between two big whales that were trying to protect it. We had an eight-millimeter French army rifle from World War I, basically a hunting rifle, with bolt action. I shot a few times at the killer whales to run them off, but as soon as we left we could see them coming back. I don't know what happened to that whale calf.

Unidentified Flying Object

Another time on the *Sea Breeze II*, I saw what I think was a UFO. This was probably around 1960, on one of the last tuna trips I made. We'd been fishing off Eureka, and there was pretty heavy fishing, so we had almost a full load of tuna. But a hard southeast wind came up so the tuna slacked off. So we started heading up to Coos Bay to be up there the next morning. There were probably a hundred boats out in that area jigging tuna and albacore.

When we got up it was just breaking day and we started trawling. I got on the back deck so I could steer the boat to change course to look for bird schools. Birds go underneath the water to feed on small fish, and sometimes albacore would be underneath the boat, feeding on the small fish too.

I saw something shining, approaching us. It looked like a UFO, just as they were described in books and newspaper articles. This thing comes up, glistening, a kind of saucer, or two saucers: one turned upside down over another right side up. It had a band of windows around it, just like in photographs I'd seen taken by people who had observed them before.

Roy Davis and a guy named Jim were fishing with me. Jim was down icing the fish we had caught the night before. "Come up here and see what's out here in the sky!" I called. I called Roy over too. We looked at it and one of us said, "I've read the stories and I didn't believe them, but it sure looks like a UFO."

Two other boats were up to the north, maybe two to three miles from us. I called them on the radio and asked them if they'd seen it, and they said "yes." You couldn't tell how far away it was. It was up off the water at about a 45-degree angle off the surface. But I couldn't guess the height straight up and the distance out. It stayed there about ten minutes, and then it just disappeared.

I didn't see the other boats until about a year later in Coos Bay. They were local boats and I talked to them then about it when they happened to be in dry dock the same time we were, at Hillstrom Shipyard. One guy said, "I think they come up out of the water!"

The military didn't want to answer our questions. They said that we saw a mirage. I think there is something to it but I don't know where they come from. There is a description in Genesis about it, and in John, Jesus says, "And other sheep I have, which are not of this fold, them also I must bring." I don't know what that really means, whether that is about Jews or something else, like UFOs. You could interpret it various ways. It's open for discussion.

I tried shrimp fishing after learning about what the Californians were doing, but the price for shrimp was 10¢ a pound and I thought I could do better at bottom trawling. I designed a beam trawl and had it built for the boat at Hillstrom's in Marshfield (now Coos Bay), but the Fish Commission only allowed beam trawls, not the ones used in the Gulf of Mexico for shrimp.

I fished one season with it. I wrote a letter and spoke with the Fish Commissioner and they exempted the net, like they do in Mexico. I ordered it from Mississippi, I think it was.

We were gone constantly, up to Cape Lookout off Tillamook and down the coast to California. I delivered to both Newport and Astoria. Up to ten or fifteen women would be picking those shrimp. The canneries only paid for the big ones but our mesh sorted them pretty good. Then I hung up the shrimp net at 96 fathoms on a sunken tugboat off Depoe Bay and decided it was a good time to quit shrimping. The net is probably still in that mud hole.

Later, in 1961, a fellow named Art Paris took the *Sea Breeze II* to Kodiak to fish Dungeness and at the same time to test the king crab fishery we'd heard about. It looked promising so my thoughts turned north to Alaska and back to crabbing.

Eventually I sold the *Sea Breeze II*. In 1969 I sold 25% of it to Craig Cochran. Two years later we sold it entirely to Jack Holt.

The King and Winge, *1965*

6. The King and Winge

I bought the *King and Winge* in Seattle in 1962, and brought it down here to Newport for conversion to a crab boat. After he'd skippered it for a while, John Hall became my partner in 1968. Even though we have the same last name, we aren't related.

The *King and Winge* was a 111-foot halibut schooner built by Tom King and Al Winge in West Seattle in 1914. It was supposed to be the most modern one of its time, and was a highliner. Back then they put sails on schooners in case of emergency, because engines weren't too trustworthy, even though they were huge heavy engines. Eventually they passed laws that said they couldn't fish with dories anymore because they'd lost too many crewmen on dories.

King and Winge were boat carpenters, or "shipwrights," they call them. They built other schooners too. They made the *King and Winge* a littler longer than the rest and gave it a little bit more beam. Awhile after I got it I started a corporation here in Oregon and called it "King and Winge, Inc."

Between the time it was built to the time I bought it, it had been a bar pilot boat in the Columbia River for 27 years. It was named the *Columbia* at that time. The bar pilots rebuilt part of it.

To convert it to a crab boat, I took it to Coos Bay to Hillstrom Ship Building Company. I knew them from the *Christian* and our other boats. They didn't have a ways big enough here in Newport at that time to haul boats out of the water, so we converted it down in

The King and Winge, *1915*

Coos Bay. We lived here in Newport and drove down there and back over the weekends. We removed some staterooms to make room for the crab hold. We put watertight steel tanks in it, and a pumping system to keep the crabs alive.

There is a cycle of crabs. The Dungeness were played out down here and there wasn't any good fishing, so it was a good time to convert and go king crabbing in Alaska. I talked it over with Joyce and she said it was all right – by that time most of the kids were in college – but she still didn't particularly care for it.

We went up on the *King and Winge* in August 1963. That was the first time I fished in Alaska. I was one of the first fishermen from Oregon to go there to fish for king crab. I took my cousin Midge's husband, Howard Miller, his son Terry, and Terry's wife Stephanie. By gory, Stephanie caught a fifteen-pound halibut on a simple line she dropped off the stern!

We fished in Shelikof Strait most of the time until fall, and then we moved closer to town and caught crabs east of Kodiak Island. We fished there that fall and then we tied the boat up and came home for Christmas for a few weeks. We went back up until the last of January or February, when the days were lengthening out.

Before he entered the service, Vern also fished on the *King and Winge*, and skippered it for a while right just before he went in, in 1966. Then Chester was going to run it, but his wife got cancer and he flew home to be with her those final months. That's when John Hall started to skipper the *King and Winge*. He bought 25% of King and Winge, Inc. in 1968, and eventually he and his wife owned 50% of the corporation.

We finally sold the *King and Winge* in the 1980s, but I continued using the corporate name for some of my other fishing business activities. Today my three daughters and their children own the corporation.

In 1992, the guys who bought the *King and Winge* were off the Pribilof Islands in the Bering Sea and I think they sprung a leak. Anyway, the boat sank. The Coast Guard took the crew off, so no one was lost. But I just think, they could have pumped out the leak and saved the boat.

The Rondys

7. The Rondys

I purchased the *Rondys* back east and three crewmen brought her around in the spring of the year, in 1966 – my nephew Danny Hall (Raymond's son), Billy Williams, and Wayne Reinertsen. They had to go through the Panama Canal. The *Rondys* was 120 feet long with a thirty-foot beam. I named her after Joyce's cousin. It was a Navy freighter built in 1931 in a Navy yard in Brooklyn, New York. I converted it to a crab boat. Supposedly the Navy had some blueprints of its original construction that I could have referred to while I converted it, but when they looked for the blueprints they discovered they'd burned them.

    I bought it from a private individual in Maryland. He had used it for building asphalt highways, hauling gravel up and down an inland canal back east. It was flat bottomed and didn't have a keel on it, so it could come through shallow water to deliver closer to where the trucks were waiting. They'd shovel gravel from the boat to the trucks.

    When the *Rondys* was built for the Navy, they had poor welding rods. They overlapped the plates in longitudinal lines on the frames and put bolts in to hold them in place, and then they bolted straps over that and welded it. After that they took the bolts out and then they welded the holes shut, so there was no flex.

    Once the boat was ours, if we had fuel in the bow, some seeped out a little bit, so we welded over the holes again. When I converted it to a crab boat, I put tanks and twin engines in it. You could pull one engine ahead and one back and spin them one way or the other.

We fished the *Rondys* in the Bering Sea along the Aleutian chain. Once it was blowing pretty hard and we decided to anchor up. A crewman named Jack Holt was in the pilothouse. One of the other fellows was up forward, letting the anchor chain down. Jack leaned out and hollered, "That's enough!" and, by gory, the wind was so hard his false teeth flew out when he opened his mouth! They came loose and went out on the deck, then through the scupper and overboard. He had to use a meat grinder for his meat and anything else tough until he got a new set of teeth, when he could afford it. At Jack's funeral a few years ago, I told that story and everybody got quite a laugh out of it.

After I bought the *Rondys*, the laws of Oregon were such that I wanted to get the benefit of the Washington tax laws, and so I formed a family corporation, Rondys, Inc. We incorporated in Oregon in 1968 and in Washington in 1972. The corporation was based in Seattle. We bought a house up in Seattle, on Crown Hill. We were there about half the time after the corporation was formed.

8. My hand

It was December 6, 1966. We were in the Hillstrom shipyard in Coos Bay, working on the *Rondys*. We were close to finishing the work on converting it, putting in the steel tanks and so forth. With the cold weather there was ice on the deck and it was slippery.

I thought we'd put a pipe in from overboard into the middle of a tank so it would keep the water revolving around the edges of the tank. That way the death loss of crabs would be less. If the water revolves, the crabs keep getting enough oxygen to survive. They need oxygen, just like people.

We were installing the pipe at low tide, and we hit the end of the dock. If the water had been higher it would have been easier. But as it was, the pipe angled up and the end of it was hitting the boat and wouldn't line up with the hole where it was supposed to go through the void into the side. So I went down inside of the void and was going to lead it through. I was going to put my hand in the pipe and lift it up until it came in.

A crewman named Elroy was doing odd jobs painting down in the engine room – I paid the crew seven to eight dollars an hour to work on the boat in the off-season in the shipyard. I told Bill Hillstrom my plan and he says, "Let's do it the easy way and not bother the shipyard guys." We put a strap around the bulwarks and lifted the crane that they had for lifting steel engines – it could lift I don't know how many tons. As it lifted it rolled the boat just a little.

It was a used strap – it was rusty and its 3/8-inch steel edges were sharp – and the cable broke. I had my left hand inside the pipe and the falling pipe severed my hand. I didn't even feel it. It cut it off quickly, just like that. It was like a guillotine.

Tendons hung out of what was left of my hand, and blood spurted out. It was cut off right through the thumb and right across the bones behind my knuckles. Elroy was down below. He caught my hand from the other end of the pipe and brought the hand back up. Jonke Elfving drove me to the hospital. It was only about a half mile away.

The doctors said, "Well, what do you want to do, try to save the hand?" They could have put it on ice and sent me up to Portland with the hand to reattach it. I said, "I don't know. There are some guys who lose their hands or fingers and then their hands are constantly cold if they put them back on." I didn't want to suffer like that.

They gave me a shot and that's the last I remember before surgery. They bent the skin back over the hand and did a perfect job. It didn't hurt too much afterwards. When I woke up, three other guys were in the ward. One guy was a farmer who'd had appendicitis, another guy was older and an alcoholic, and the other guy had cancer of the rectum. They were all sicker than I was.

I stayed in the hospital three nights. When I got home, our dog Heidi – she was a mongrel, mostly Spaniel – she came up to lick my hand, and tears rolled out of her eyes!

Soon afterwards I went down to the boat here in Newport with my hand in a bandage, to check out how I did at my station up at the controls in the wheelhouse, and to check on progress of the work. The steering was about ready to go, and we had pots being built. We got loaded up and left around New Year's Day and headed across the Gulf of Alaska to the Bering Sea.

I didn't have any problem with steering the boat with one hand. I could kick in the control levers with my stub on both sides of the pilothouse. With my fishing experience it was easy to adapt, plus I had a good crew and engineer, so we didn't have any problems.

My hand healed while I was at sea and I didn't come off the boat until May. When I came down home I had the prosthesis made. They made a heavy one for work and it fit so well that I had them build a smaller, lighter one too.

I talked to a fellow who lost his hand up in Astoria and he said he tried that "Boston Claw," they called it. It could open and close artificial fingers so you could hold something. The doctors said it was critical if you were working all the time to put new batteries in, but this fellow in Astoria decided a simple one was best and that is what he returned to. That's what I got too. It is basically a hook.

The lawyers for the Hillstrom Shipyard in Coos Bay wanted to settle. We settled for $10,000, to cover what I had to pay for the prosthesis and for its maintenance down the road. They made a check out to me for $10,000 and I turned around and made a check out for $10,000 for the church they were building up here at the time, for the building fund. It's the Newport First Christian Church, the one I still attend.

Three more of my boats: The Alsea, Argosy *and* Progress

9. More boats, more partners

In 1972 Vern and I built the *Provider*, in Bellingham, at the old Post Point Marine Naval Yard. We built it in partnership with John Hall again and his wife Sue. John's family came from West Virginia and our whole family came from Kentucky, but they weren't very far apart so I believe that we were related somewhat. Anyway, construction was finished in 1973 and we each had a quarter of the boat. I never went to sea on the *Provider*, but I oversaw all the work we did on it onshore.

We had to borrow money to build the boat from the Northwest Livestock Production Credit Association. I found out about them from a rancher in eastern Oregon. It was the first marine loan that they ever made. They made loans to farmers, but they decided that they could go into marine and I was the first recipient. The loan was dated March 28, 1973. We borrowed about $560,000. We had about half of the purchase price to support the loan and we paid it off within a few years.

The *Provider* was modeled after the *Rondys* only it had better lines and it was better built. Plates were laid against each other and were welded together inside and outside. It was built out of 3/8-inch steel, braced down with center bulkheads for safety. The crab fishery had problems with a lot of boats turning over because of the shifting of the weight if you had a top load. The center bulkheads would prevent the

The Provider

weight of the crabs from shifting.

To minimize the risk of getting top-heavy, we built the *Provider* with bottom tanks and we always kept those full with fuel. We never had any problems. When the boat surveyors gave the boat the rolling chalk test, it rolled back to center quickly.

We had a hatch made to come up from the hold above deck, maybe a foot and a half or two feet high. Sometimes the boat rolled over to 45 degrees and water spilled out of the opening and flew clear across the boat, leaving one side of the hold without any water. To solve the problem, I worked with Marco, a ship building company in Seattle. They put sponsons on each side to keep the tanks in the middle, so the *Provider* was built with four tanks. They were about twenty feet long, so forty feet of the boat was tanks.

Several years later, we had the boat cut in two and they put in more tanks. The engines were in the stern of the boat and we restructured the engine room, making the boat longer, from 117 feet long to 137 feet long. That is what it still is.

The *Atlantico*

In 1973 I bought the *Atlantico* in partnership will Bill Jacobson, 50/50, from a meat packing plant based in Chicago. The *Atlantico* was built a few years before in Alabama, to shrimp off the Amazon River Delta, which it did for several years. It was in the Gulf of Mexico when we bought it, in Brownsville, Texas. A fellow named Larry Armour owned the shipyard and represented the owners. There was a time during the gas shortage that lawyers for the Exxon Company and various community representatives were all in Houston. Joyce, Bill and I were there for about a week.

I offered $180,000 for the boat and put the money in the bank in escrow, but they said Larry Armour was out of the country and they couldn't reach him. Finally, after about a week, I said, "I'll give you 24 hours and after that we will pull the money out and buy another boat at another place I've been." I'd looked at several boats overseas too.

After a couple of hours we got a call in our hotel room. "Come over and sign the papers," the person said. That closed the deal right there.

The Atlantico

At that time there were boats being built from the west coast down to the Gulf of Mexico and the cheapest boats were down south. Labor cost about half what it did on the west coast, and steel did too. At that time steel was being produced in the steel mills of Alabama.

They had quite an advantage down there because the standard of living was lower. The food in restaurants and motels cost less. It wasn't expensive for us to be there.

The *Atlantico* had fished down in Brazil. Boats from countries that bordered Brazil fished down there, in Brazilian waters, for shrimp. American boats too.

When Brazil started to enforce the 200-mile limit out from their shores, they closed that to other countries. American skippers just pulled their boats into the company processing plant, tied up, and came back to the States. Then they hired other guys to bring the boats back up north, mostly to the States. That's what happened to the *Atlantico*, but it was brought to Mexico. *Mar Atlantico* was its Spanish name.

After we bought it, Bill brought it through the Panama Canal. It shrimped off Kodiak from 1974 to 1978, and then crabbed, longlined for halibut, fished for salmon, and tendered herring in Alaska. I ran it for the 1974 fall king crab fishery. When we were fishing, the live crabs that were big enough went right in the tanks. The ones that were too small went back overboard. Unloading the bigger boats with steel tanks, we washed them down and cleaned off the barnacles each time we delivered. There was no smell except the saltwater smell.

When you unload the crab, they don't make any noise, except for the clicking of their claws against each other. They're slow, especially the king crab. The Dungeness crabs are smaller and faster. When you handle them, you reach back underneath and get your thumb positioned so you don't get pinched.

Eventually I turned the *Atlantico* entirely over to Bill and he got another fellow, Mike Woodley, to run it part-time in the early 1990s. Eventually Mike owned 25% of it. One time the bottom of the hull got dented, so we sold the rest of it to Mike at a reduced price, in 2006.

The *Baron*

We bought the *Baron* in 1973 too, in partnership with Brian Elfving, son of Jonke and grandson of Abe Elfving, who designed the *Tupper* years before – we knew the whole family pretty well. The *Baron* was designed as a tugboat originally. It was around ninety feet long. Brian Elfving got a couple of other guys to bring it around from the Gulf of Mexico, through the Panama Canal. It took about a month. It was designed for Gulf fishing, had two outriggers and a small net on each. I never actually fished on it myself.

The *Baron* fished shrimp up in Alaska for a while, but we didn't have heavy enough gear for the amount of shrimp. Down in the Gulf of Mexico they didn't catch any amount of shrimp like they did up in Alaska. They could hardly pull the gear in, so we brought it in to the shipyard and overhauled it for crabbing.

At that time, they wouldn't insure insure a boat if you took your wife or children on it, but some guys wanted their wives there, especially skippers, because they were away for quite a while. Once the *Baron* was ready for crabbing, we hired a skipper. He wanted to bring along his wife and baby, but I told him the insurance wouldn't allow it.

I wasn't aware of it, but he took his wife and baby anyway. They slept in a wider bunk, all together. He went to sleep and he ran it aground on its maiden voyage crabbing. Thankfully, it was on a sandy area, so they all got off without getting hurt.

The boat was in such bad condition that the insurance company declared it a total loss. The Coast Guard shot shells into it and sank it offshore. After that John Hall designed a watch alarm system and I made it a policy for all my vessels. The Seattle hull insurance pools later adopted this watch alarm system to be used whenever boats are underway.

All our boats were insured through five different hull insurance pools in Seattle. I was paying for regular insurance here in Oregon, but some fellows in Seattle got me in as a member of the insurance pools up there, and it cost a lot less. Members pay heavily for a few years, and then it tapers off. If you have an accident they take money out of your account, and if there isn't enough to cover the accident they dip into the other accounts in the insurance pool. They can vote somebody out of the pool if they aren't acting safely.

We also had "Protection and Indemnity" insurance for crewmembers' accidents. We called it "P&I" insurance. It's liability insurance for personal injuries or illness while fishing.

The *Progress*

Rondys, Inc. built the *Progress* in 1975 and later it became a partnership with F.C. Robison – "Beanie" is what we call him. It was built at Hansen Boat Company in Steamboat Slough, about a mile from Marysville, Washington. It was 114 feet long and designed as a combination vessel to both crab and trawl. We went down and loaded pots on in Seattle, got fuel and groceries, and left right after July 4 for Dutch Harbor. When the boat was new, we fished for bairdi crab, also known as tanner crab.

The wheelhouse was forward on the *Progress*, so we had to use mirrors to view the crew at work on the decks behind us. (On the *Rondys* and *Provider*, the houses were aft so you'd see the deck looking ahead without mirrors.) On the *Progress*, we also had to use mirrors to pull up alongside the buoys to haul the gear. You could tell when the crabs were running the stream or if they were moving across the other way.

As we were hauling, the mirrors enabled us to see the guys when they were ready to dump the pots out. When they dumped them I pushed a button and blew a horn. Crewmen hollered out the number of crabs to a pot and I'd write it down in a log.

Beanie didn't go on the *Progress* until about the second year. The first year he was a member of the crew. I put him on as skipper eventually, in 1978. That was the last year I actively fished.

I left to take care of the other boats that were building the business. Beanie still is master of the *Progress*. His first year as master was a big year. He had a million pounds of heavy fishing. He went out for 36 hours and loaded up the boat. He had to wait a day or two to unload because the processors were too full.

All Alaskan Seafoods

All Alaskan Seafoods started in 1976. Ten guys were in it to start, including me – thirteen eventually. We bought a floating processor ship that was tied up in Tacoma and had just been left there. There is quite a history to it.

These kinds of boats were built during World War II as transport boats. They were about 400-foot boats with a forty- or fifty-foot beam. They delivered frozen foods to different ports in Europe to the U.S. armed forces. After the war they were fixed up and converted to processors because they had refrigeration in the holds.

The guy who owned this particular boat was trying to apply for financing so he could process fish up in Alaska. The boat had already been moved from Astoria, Oregon to Tacoma, Washington. But he ran up some big bills, so he decided to auction it off.

I went up to Tacoma and met him and went to the auction. I had my accountant from Newport with me and had $200,000 available to bid on it. These others guys, nine of them altogether, bid on it too. It went up to $200,000 and I backed down. These other guys got it, but afterwards one of them called me up and said, "Would you like to be a partner with us? There is a tenth spot." I said yes.

We named it the *All Alaskan* and converted it into a crab processor. Because it was a processor it was a marine vessel (M/V), not a fishing vessel (F/V), like most of my other boats. Eventually Rondys,

Inc. owned 16% of the *All Alaskan*, and Vern and I each owned 4%.

The *All Alaskan* was the mother ship. Later on, in 1982 or '83, we bought a processing plant in Kodiak called the Star of Kodiak, which we sold to Tyson Seafoods in 1994. In 1986 we bought a processing barge called the *Northern Alaskan*, and from 1999 to 2011 we owned Barnacle Point Shipyard in Ballard. We had many other business ventures too.

We bought herring in Prince William Sound but we lost that fishery because of the Exxon Valdez oil spill in 1989. Many of our operations were suspended. Now the Sound has recovered and it is just as good as it ever was.

We finally divested everything by 2011. One of our subsidiaries finally got some money from the Exxon Valdez settlement that same year, in 2011 – over twenty years after the spill!

The *Argosy* and the *Alsea*

In 1985, Rondys, Inc. bought two boats called the *Aries* and the *Taurus* that were built by a fellow named Bill White. We renamed the *Aries* the *Argosy* and the *Taurus* the *Alsea*, after the river in Waldport.

The *Argosy* was on auction. Buying that was simple. It's not that boats available at auction are in bad condition necessarily, it's that the owners get over-extended. They try to increase too much too fast. They build too many boats and go bankrupt. This happened especially after the U.S. got the Russians and Japanese out of American waters.

An outfit from South America bought the other boat at auction, but they had to let it go because they went bankrupt too, so then we bought it. That was the *Alsea*.

We bought the *Argosy* in partnership with Tom Moe, and the *Alsea* with a fellow named Tim Gerding. They were both combination crabber/trawler boats and focused on the emerging pollock fishery in the Bering Sea. Eventually we widened them with sponsons. They're both still in operation.

I've had lots of business partners in my life. I believe it's the Christian way. I've read about people of faith and how they do business. The J.C. Penney founder originally called his stores the Golden Rule because that was his philosophy.

Safeway started in American Falls, Idaho, where I was born.

The founder was a Christian and he believed in expanding by keeping a narrow profit margin. He put stores in lots of small towns and took in partners with him to manage the business. He could see that the ones who were responsible and energetic would do a good job.

So why not work in the fisheries in the same way? If you get people on deck that are competent and they start at the bottom of the ladder and work up, the higher people see it.

Safety is the first thing you want. Your lives are at stake and after that the boat, but the lives of the people and the families that they support are most important. That's why you make the boat seaworthy and have safety features, and teach them about it. That's why I wouldn't allow alcohol on the boats.

In the Bible, Moses tried to arbitrate problems among the people, and he couldn't do it. His father-in-law came to him and said, "You can't do this alone. You have to split this out in tens. Put other people in charge to have authority in certain fields." Moses had to do that because he wasn't capable of doing it all by himself.

It's the same trying to help others on crab boats. On deck, it takes young fellows that are husky and physically fit. They don't do very well if they are incapacitated and they can't do their share. In the engine room, you can rotate the ones who have mechanical experience. You are helping them go up the ladder because later on they can get licenses and get on larger boats.

You put people where you think they can serve best. You allocate authority and make sure the knowledge is passed on so that everyone is dispensable. But even though everyone is dispensable, I was on call at all times – I didn't mind it. But you can't compensate for people, either. Some people are more valuable than others, and not all have the same talents. I had a high school friend, Franklin Tabor. He was a good cartoonist. That was his talent.

One of my longtime partners is John Hall. We've gone into other businesses too, not just fishing. In 1984 he got in a terrible accident, not on a boat, but in an airplane. It was up at the airstrip in Ekuk, Alaska, an Indian village about twenty miles downriver from Dillingham. It was across from where they packed salmon, on a tidal flat. They had to fly in cash from Dillingham to buy salmon once a week, in suitcases full of $100 bills.

Anyway, they came up the runway and the wheels caught the bulkhead on the runway. The wheels came up, pushed John up through the roof of the plane, and broke his back. Two vertebrae were shattered.

No one else was hurt. John was sitting alongside the co-pilot, but the co-pilot was all right. John was the only one hurt. His back is healed now but he has two pieces of stainless steel up each side of his spinal column, so part of his back is stiff. He now uses his talents not in fishing but running the San-I-Pak Pacific company for us in Tracy, California.

Crew size

On the larger boats we'd have more crewmen than we did on the smaller boats in the early days. We usually had four or five. With more crewmen we could work round the clock. We had one guy sleeping in his bunk for four or five hours, and rotate through the guys to get through the gear.

Some crewmen fished with me a short time. Some told me ahead of time they'd only fish for so long, like Scott McMullen. He was a crewman who fished for me for a year or two before he left to buy a small shrimp boat to fish out of Astoria. Now he teaches fishing safety at the community college there, and also works for a cable company that lays cables across the ocean bottom. He keeps fishermen informed of where the cables are. He cuts their nets off a cable if they hang up on it so they don't damage it. The company reimburses the fishermen for their nets.

Other crewmen fished with me longer, up to seven years, when I was a captain. They'd get older and skipper a boat, get experience with that and eventually buy a boat, sometimes with a partner. I encouraged them to do that, to go out on their own. A lot of times they even borrowed money from me to do that. I did that for lots of fellows. I was happy to do it.

*Family portrait, 1960.
Standing, left to right: Bonnie, Vern, Joyce, Janet.
Seated: Me and Margaret*

10. Family business

Vern graduated from high school in 1963, and went on to college for three years at Oregon State University in Corvallis. During that time he fished some seasons on the *King and Winge*. I asked him one time what he learned at college. He said he learned that it's easier to loan money than to collect it. After that he joined the Navy for four years, and served three years in Vietnam, patrolling the rivers.

About the time Vern came back from the Navy, I gave my nephew Danny and some of his friends jobs as crewmen, and started Vern in the engine room on the *Rondys*. My brother Chester was going to skipper the *King and Winge* about the same time. I told Joyce, "There's something wrong with Wilma. She doesn't look good at all." I was right. Chester drove the *King and Winge* to Dutch Harbor when he learned that his wife was diagnosed with terminal cancer, so he flew home. They lived in Eureka, California and had three sons. Wilma soon died from pancreatic cancer. Later, Chet went on to buy his own boat.

When Chester had to look after Wilma before she died, we got John Hall to run the *King and Winge*. Before that, John had been a crewman on Clifford Hall's boat, the *Tiffany*. (Clifford is John's uncle but they aren't related to me.) Later on I made John part owner of the *King and Winge*.

After Vern came back from the service and worked for a few years on the *Rondys*, I turned 50% of Rondys, Inc. over to him with the

My children in 2005.
Left to right: Margaret, Vern, Janet, Bonnie

understanding that the girls would have all of King and Winge, Inc. and other entities. On evaluation, up until then he was getting most of the family business. He was brought into the business earlier than they were and I wanted them to catch up. I've tried hard to be fair. They are all four involved now, somehow or other. Now I'm out of it. I don't need the money.

Margaret went to college for public health management. Then she worked in the healthcare industry, but I don't think she felt she was getting promoted fast enough. I offered her a job in the fishing industry, in accounting and insurance and other areas. I told her my business was getting to be too much for me to handle. We had our accountant here in Newport, but that wasn't enough. We needed somebody to do the Rondys, Inc. books. We worked her in gradually and she picked it up and she did a really good job. She started in 1985. She's taken care of the *Alsea*, the *Argosy*, and the *Progress* for over 25 years. Recently Vern took over the books for the *Progress*, but Margaret's still the main bookkeeper for Rondys, Inc. She looks after all the businesses and attends a lot of meetings.

For a while I gave enough money every year to grandchildren

and great-grandchildren so that they'd have an education. I gave probably 20% of my income every year to them. Now I just give them stock because I don't have the cash resources – I'm only in the stock market. I keep track of my stocks every day on a pad of paper.

I've also given about six million dollars to Boise Bible College, and student enrollment increased from about 180 to 210 students.

I started tithing in church after high school. Bill Parsons and his wife took their youngest son (not his brother, my best friend Arleon) on a mission to Indonesia and they stayed ten years. I tithed to their mission a couple times a year for many years. Over the years I tithed at least 10%. Now I tithe probably 20%. But I still have a lot left for my family.

The *Vanguard*

Vern had the *Vanguard* built in Coos Bay in 1980, with a partner. Then I took the partner's place, and Vern and I hired a skipper, a fellow from Bulgaria named Stoian Ianov. He had jumped ship off a Russian processing ship in Coos Bay when it came in for supplies. Eventually Stoian became a partner in the *Vanguard* too.

I told Stoian that he should get a boat of his own after he became a U.S. citizen, and he did. My company, King and Winge, Inc. bought his share in the *Vanguard* back, in about 2002, so he could buy a boat on his own. He's been fishing his own boat for several years. He's a really good fisherman.

The *Sourdough*

In 1987, Rondys, Inc. bought the *Northern Endeavor* at a sheriff's auction, and we re-named it the *Sourdough*. It was about 175 feet long. Vern hired a skipper to run it. It fished for about a year or two. It had a two-cycle General Motors diesel engine and a huge reduction gear in it.

Then another man, who had an engineering degree, ran it and he didn't drain the water out and it leaked. Usually you open up a valve and let the water out so it doesn't run into the sump of the cylinder. But he didn't, and water came up to the top of the cylinder and broke the head on it. The *Vanguard* towed it from Dutch Harbor down to Newport here and we put in a new engine, hydraulics and everything.

The Sourdough

After All Alaskan Seafood's Russian joint venture was over, I heard the *Sourdough* was in North Korea for a while, but now I don't know where it's gone. It can't fish in the U.S. anymore. It can only haul passengers or something like that. The *Rondys* was fishing in South America somewhere, but now they say it's in Gray's Harbor, Washington, where they use it for hauling waste products out to sea.

Russian joint venture

The *All Alaskan* ran aground in the Pribilofs in 1987. We replaced it in 1995 with a boat called the *Rybak Chichuski* that was built in Poland for the Russians. The year before, in 1994, we formed a partnership with a Russian company to crab in the Sea of Okhotsk as part of a fleet of ten boats. The fleet included two of our catcher boats, the *Rondys* and the *Sourdough*. Other All Alaskan Seafood shareholders owned the other eight boats. The *Rybak* was the mother ship. We completed the expected ten-year contract in less than six years, and the boats became the property of the Russians. Eventually we bought the *Rondys* back from them, but without its coastwise endorsement. Then we sold it again.

We knew that by going to Russia we would lose our U.S. fishing history that would have been used for the crab rationalization program. I think we lost in the long run. If you fished in Russia you had to register your boat there, but you couldn't bring a boat back in the U.S. with a Russian registry, at least not with fishing rights.

July 22, 2000

11. Loss and joy

Joyce died suddenly, on May 4, 1999. She had a heart attack. We'd been on an RV trip the week before and we had a lot of things to take care of when we got back, including making some repairs on the RV. We took it into an automotive shop.

When it was ready, Joyce drove me to pick it up and bring it back home. We still lived on Abbey Street, where we raised our kids. She was going to have a session with a dog trainer, along with some other people and their dogs, at the elementary school, right up the street from where I live now. It was almost summertime so they met outside.

The dog was named Chipper. Joyce wanted the dog, but I didn't care for it. My cousin and his wife had the same kind of dog, turns out from the same litter of Silky Terriers. They are little dogs that were bred over in Britain to chase weasels and foxes through hollow logs and tunnels. They are really quick and small. Anyway, my cousin's wife was at the school for the dog training class with her dog at the same time as Joyce.

On the way to the RV place Joyce said, "I'm getting a headache and I haven't got any aspirin with me." She used to take half an aspirin each day to prevent a heart attack, and extra when she had a headache.

After she dropped me off, she went to the dog obedience class, where they taught the dogs to sit, stay, come, heel and so forth. Suddenly Joyce said, "I'm getting dizzy," and she bent down and told Chipper to lie down and stay down.

With Joyce

The trainer was a cardiac nurse from the hospital. She told Joyce to lie down while she called 911. The emergency vehicle took about ten minutes to arrive, and during that time Joyce passed out. They rushed her to the hospital, but she died on the way and they couldn't bring her back.

They called me up and I talked to the doctor. He said they tried to bring her back for a half hour, but to no avail. He said that if they had brought her back she'd be in bad shape. After that amount of time there probably would have been significant brain injury.

Joyce was a good wife to me. She had to be when I was fishing. She was a good mother too. She took good care of the kids – she kept them clean and in school.

She was active in the community too. She was our church secretary and the Sunday school supervisor. She was a youth group advisor and a 4H leader. She became a good photographer and took lots of pictures of our family, both slides and 8mm movies. Once the kids were gone, she moved to Kodiak when I was fishing there, and made friends there. She became very independent and had a mind of her own!

Joyce's funeral was not a sad affair like many funerals. A pianist played her favorite revival music, and the high school band played wearing the new uniforms she bought for them. Lots of people told stories about her, including how she taught a handful of boys how to drive at the abandoned airport, and stories about her own fast driving. There were several women there from the Olsonville Sewing Club. Joyce belonged to that club for many years, not just because she was a good seamstress, but because they were good friends. She sewed a lot of the kids' clothes as they grew up.

Kathleen was acquainted with Joyce through our church, and was sad when Joyce died. Kathleen and I started going together the following year. She was a widow. I was lonesome and so was she – we needed each other.

On our first date we went out to dinner and had Chinese food. After that we sat together in church. I'd lean over and whisper, "This will probably cause a lot of tongues to start wagging."

Kathleen and I dated some more. We usually went out for a meal. Finally we decided to get married, and were on July 22, 2000. All my kids think I've got a good wife again. She is a good cook, is very kind, and takes really good care of me.

Joyce was a believer, and so is Kathleen. That's something they have in common, and it's really important to me.

With round crab pots, 2012

12. Perfecting crab pots

Dungeness crabbing

Back in the 1930s, a lot of pots were built to fit the size of the boats. Most of the crab boats were trollers, about twenty to thirty feet long. They fished in the bays along the coast, especially around the river mouths. Fishermen didn't really crab in the ocean yet.

Because of the regulation against using crab pots in the bays, the fishermen used crab rings, which have a single big ring at the top with a double bottom and are smaller than the regular pots. The rings measure about thirty inches across the top and about eighteen inches at the bottom. The crabs get tangled in the web in the double bottom and cling to the side as the ring is lifted. The fisherman needs to pull fast so the crabs can't escape. Today, tourists can rent these same crab rings for bay crabbing.

When I was a boy growing up on the Alsea Bay, I baited a crab ring and carefully set it in the water to keep the lines from getting tangled. I found daybreak to be the best time to watch the crabs' behavior before I caught them, and I learned that they are cautious animals. I stood about thirty feet away on a sand spit on the west side of the water where the crabs were, so my shadow wouldn't scare the crabs away.

About 1937, my brothers and I were fishing out of Charleston, Oregon, with South Slough and Coos Bay behind us. It was a popular place for bay crabbing. But when we realized that there were a lot of crabs out in the ocean, we needed better pots to catch them. We started to build our own pots. That's when it came in handy that we'd been trained in knitting pots. We bought the steel frames – they only cost about three or four dollars – and we pulled the copper wire webbing tight so the crabs couldn't get out. We used old crankshafts out of automobiles for the weights on the bottom. Later on we bought steel bar rejects from Jewish merchants in Portland.

Once we designed and built our own pots, overnight we started catching more crabs than the bay crabbers. They couldn't compete with us. After setting the pots, we went out about daylight and we'd have eight or ten pots chock full, and by afternoon we'd be back in. We built lots of pots in the winter, up to sixty to eighty pots to replace the ones we lost.

Some people credit me and my brothers with designing and developing round crab pots, the circular kind that are used now up and down the west coast for Dungeness crab. I didn't invent them – a lot of guys began using them about the same time – but my brothers and I helped develop them more.

Originally, some of the pots other folks experimented with were square, eighteen inches to two feet high. But with the short lines, the swells lifted the pots and they ended up washed up on the beach, sanded under. You need to leave extra line, depending on the depth, so this doesn't happen. We used pumps from the Navy salvage store to get them out of the sand. So we made our pots shorter, only 10½ to twelve inches high, and of course, round.

We tried different size meshes. We replaced the cotton mesh with copper wire mesh, but our catch went down. Then we discovered that copper causes electrolysis, which gets hot and repels crabs. The first time we heard about it was from Abe Elfving. He called it "galvanic action," which happens on the boat shaft. We put zinc in the hull to prevent this.

A fellow who sold stainless steel, Warren Gilbert, told us what some fishermen in Grays Harbor did. They used stainless knit web. We then experimented using steel frames coated with rubber to protect the metal from electrolysis and corrosion. We tried it and that did the trick. We caught more crabs on the *Tupper* and *Mary Frances* than the rest of the fleet altogether.

We also tried different weight bars and made the pots heavier. We increased the weight from about seventy pounds to up to 145 pounds. We caught a lot more crabs that way. We beat the socks off the other guys.

The best crab pots are the ones with an entrance on the ground level. The tunnel the crabs came through tapered in from each side of a round double ring, and left a vault for the original pots two feet high and about 34 inches in diameter. There were six uprights between the two sides that were a little narrower, and there was a tunnel within a tunnel that sloped up to the top. At first, they didn't have any triggers in them, so the crabs could escape.

Harold Hunter invented the first triggers that locked the crabs in. Triggers are two wires that hang down in the tunnels. There are weights in the bottom and lines attached to the top and to the bottom that pulled the triggers up on an angle. The triggers hung from the top rim near where they were attached. We were the first to put them on our boats. We thought it was important that small crabs escape to reproduce.

When we put triggers in the pots, the ones that Harold invented, we tested a pot first by putting it in the live box. We baited it, put a few crabs in with it, and pushed the triggers open. It was only about six feet deep so you could watch how they reacted. It took a while for the crabs to enter the pot, but once one went in, the others would follow. We also put in soft crabs that weren't quite hard enough to put on the market and fed them until they gained weight. We saw how fast they gained weight. It was a slow process. It takes all summer in the live box until they were saleable in late September or October.

Eventually we made bigger pots, about 42 inches in diameter. Just two inches more in diameter increased the capacity quite a bit. We didn't have much competition for a few years. We fished further away in the winter, up to Cape Perpetua. We fished about 25% more than other boats. Most of them didn't even start crabbing in Coos Bay until April.

Years later, out of Newport, when we got the pots perfected, we fished 500 to 1,000 of them on the *Sea Breeze II* and brought in more than a million pounds of crab in some seasons.

King crabbing

When we first went to Alaska on the *King and Winge* in 1963, there was a forty-pot limit (eventually they removed that limit). In the spring of '64, we went back to using square pots so we could transport them more easily. They were trapezoids, actually. They were eight feet square on the bottom, four feet square on the top, and about thirty inches high. There were plastic tunnels two feet wide that ran down the inside on two sides. The herring that we used for bait was put just underneath the tunnels to draw them.

At first we designed them so the bottoms could swing down when we unloaded, but it took too much time to detach the bottoms. Then we designed a pot with a removable lid, but that was too slow and difficult. We finally decided that square pots were best for convenience sake. The inverted shape allowed better stacking. The *King and Winge* was very narrow, so how the pots fit was important.

One theory is that crab will walk along one side of a square pot and keep walking away from the pot, but with a round pot they'll walk around it until they figure out how to get in. We had to use good bait, such as mature herring that was really oily and smelly to overcome that because crabs are driven mostly by hunger.

We also tried different crab escapes, systems to allow undersized crabs to get out, but they didn't work. Eventually we learned that changing the web size is better for escapement. Rather than the web being small all over with only one place for small crabs to escape, like in Dungeness pots, we just made the web bigger. That way the legal crabs stayed trapped in the pot but the smaller crabs got out more easily. The webbing hung on the inner frames. We also put zinc in the pots to combat electrolysis in the steel frames.

Smaller king crab boats out of Seldovia made pots round like big Dungeness pots, maybe five feet across. They had two timbers run out past the stern of the boat, six to eight feet long, to carry them and keep them from rolling off the deck. They hauled maybe ten pots at the most. That practice died out in a few years.

The Dungeness fishery still uses round pots because they work better in Pacific currents. The king and opilio crab fisheries use square pots because there is more room with square pots on larger boats, and they stack more tightly together, so deck space is used more efficiently.

13. Crab peculiarities

Crabs sense the current. Whatever way the current is running, they follow it. At the north side of Alsea Bay, right in the mouth, there is a long spit out to the channel. The water is about knee deep and you could see the crabs clearly.

We had the line on the sunny side of the spit, the east side where the sun climbed up in the morning. The tides came in on average six minutes later every day, and then earlier, from full moon to full moon again every month.

I observed the crabs in the shallow water, there on the sunny side of the spit, and did experiments. I would throw out a crab ring, then watch the crabs and see how they reacted to the bait, not just the currents. They were scary to me at first. They moved pretty fast with their legs but they didn't want to get on that ring. Finally one would take the bait and get trapped in the ring, and then they they'd all go in, like "Follow the Leader."

The kind of crab we caught in Oregon is Dungeness crab. They are larger out in the ocean than in the bays. They are the same species but the smaller crabs come into shallower water, usually in the spring. They actually lose their shell, grow a new shell, and expand their size. After four or five years they were up to marketable size.

There is a line on the back of a crab that splits open to reveal a mass of gelatin. It is pulled right back through the joints of the legs. At that time they are susceptible to other forms of marine life feeding on them. It takes several months for the shells to harden up – it is usually November before they are very good. Eventually they get so old they quit molting.

In Alaska we caught mostly king crabs, but on the *Progress* we also caught bairdi crabs (also known as tanner crabs). Bairdi crabs can live up to a decade and adults can weigh up to four pounds.

For the king crabs we had individual pots, lines, and buoys – different from longlining. They longline for orange deep sea crabs, also called brown king crabs, on the deep water coral banks, meaning there is one long line of pots, maybe 100 to 250 fathoms deep. The coral banks run offshore down the Aleutian chain. Conservationists don't allow the coral to be disturbed. Sometimes the crab move off the coral themselves, but they don't stay away long. These orange crabs are a different crab. They have a lot of horns all over their shells, not like the red king crabs. The *Sourdough* used to fish for orange king crabs – or brown crabs, same thing.

Crabs lay eggs, and when the larvae or tadpoles emerge, sometimes they get on the lines or get eaten by other fish. One thing lives on the other – that's the food chain. When king crabs mature they have a little tail with a spike on it, but they don't have horns like orange or brown crabs.

King crabs have longer legs than Dungeness crabs, and king crabs get big in Alaska. By gory, I think we caught one crab in Shelikof Strait that weighed 33 pounds!

Dungeness crabs grow bigger in Alaska than they do here in Oregon. Once in a while we'd get a crab down here that weighed two or three pounds. Up there they average four to five pounds. I mean average, so some are bigger. They are bigger because they get better feed. They go into hibernation when the water gets cold enough. They burrow down in the seabed and hibernate like bears do on land.

Now they are starting to raise crabs in the laboratory in Kodiak, like salmon farming. They put king crab larvae in salt water in the lab, and then put them back in the ocean to fend for themselves and mature. I hope it works.

14. Fishing politics

Financing fishing boats

When we bought the *Rondys*, the price was $180,000 and I needed financing. I thought I could borrow money from a lumber company that I'd lent money to before, when they needed it. When I asked the fellow who first said he would loan me the money, this time he said "no" because the rest of his family refused to honor his word. Then I asked the Bureau of Commercial Fisheries for a loan, but they denied me too.

So in the spring of 1966, I went to Washington, D.C. to visit Oregon's U.S. Representative Edith Green, to explain my problem. She was an advocate for education, the first woman in Congress who got federal money for college student loans. I told her how fishermen couldn't get guaranteed loans from the government like other industries could. She set me up with an appointment to see the Chairman of the Merchant Marine Fisheries Committee the next day, over in the Rayburn Building. He was a representative from New Jersey.

The pages ran me over to his office. The crosswalk had a roof over it, and the route must have been a quarter of a mile long. I explained my problem again to him: I needed money for a boat to fish crab in the Bering Sea and I couldn't get a loan. I needed the money to feed Americans. I asked, "Why couldn't fishing boats qualify for guaranteed loans?"

I also told him the Japanese and Russians were fishing for crabs in the Bering Sea, but there were no American boats fishing there. It was an unused natural resource for us.

He said, "You're not a recognized industry." I asked, "Why not?" He said, "Because you're not what they call a 'peanut crop,' like the wheat growers." They were subsidized. He said, "If you're not subsidized, you're not recognized as an industry," and I said, "Well, fishing and agriculture have a lot in common."

He finally told me to go home and write him a letter so that it was all on paper. So that's what I did. I came home and wrote the letter he asked for, about what I wanted to do and how much money I needed for converting the boat to a Bering Sea crabber. This included replacing the equipment (generators and so forth), making watertight tanks, and installing safety features. Joyce typed the letter up and we sent it back.

About ten days later I received a telegram from this chairman. It said I could use this telegram as authorization to get a loan that was guaranteed by the U.S. government. I took it to the Bank of Newport and got my loan. By gory, it came through!

Eventually this loan program became available for all fishermen. It benefited guys in the Gulf of Mexico to build shrimp boats that could go clear down past Mexico, more than those of us who built boats for use in Alaska. By then most boats being built had steel hulls.

Then a fellow up in Kodiak named Ralph Jones gave me a brochure about Capital Construction Funds (CCFs). I learned that the Merchant Marine Act of 1936 created CCFs for all kinds of vessels, mostly for use in the oil industry, but fishing boats weren't included. A 1970 amendment to the Merchant Marine Act extended CCFs to include fishing vessels, but not many fishing boats I knew used them. It sounded like a good deal. With a CCF, taxes can be deferred on income deposited into a fund that's used for the replacement of vessels. I think CCFs were first used by supply ships to Europe, then by oil company boats in the Gulf of Mexico, then by tug boat companies, and now finally by fishing boats.

After paying back my loan for the *Rondys*, we put money into a CCF account that helped us build the *Provider* in 1972. Like I said, we borrowed the rest from the Northwest Livestock Production Credit Association. Now they've changed their name or merged with some other business, but they've become a big lending bank for many fishermen.

CCFs helped later on to replace the Japanese and Russian fleets, after the Magnuson Act of 1976 established a 200-mile fishery conservation zone. CCFs enabled more American fishermen to improve their boats and fish further out in the ocean. Japanese boats caught crab in nets and piled them in their boats and wouldn't process them until the next day or two, so the crab was poor quality. American boats delivered live crabs to the processors and they were processed when they were alive, so you got top quality. There was no comparison.

Oregon Sea Grant Advisory Board

After I retired I was on the Oregon Sea Grant Advisory Board, from 1978 to 1985. In Newport there were seven or eight of us on that board. We met every few months. Different guys would do it for a few years and retire. Most of them were old and had time, like me. I was here at home by then. Our role was just to listen in and advocate.

The chairman was a fellow from Oregon State University (OSU), because OSU established the Oregon Sea Grant. They're an integrated program of marine research, education and public engagement.

One concern we had was oysters. They brought oysters from Japan to be used as seed oysters in Netarts Bay, where they had an oyster plant. They heated salt water at the plant so the shells could grow the oyster spat or larvae. They scattered the shells from the formed oysters so they didn't have to bring oysters over from Japan anymore.

I had another concern. I kept advocating that more research vessels be sent to Alaska, because Japanese and Russians knew more about the history of fishing in Alaska than the U.S. did. But they didn't follow my advice. They didn't send any research boats north to Alaska until much later.

People that were graduating wrote their theses on other research, on their ideas about currents and water temperatures. I watched them for years and read their diaries.

I thought that they were completely wrong. I thought the Japanese Current on the bottom was so deep that the temperature stayed the same. I told the president of OSU about it. I said that the top current goes out far and that when you have a steady wind out of the south it will create a top current that will be stronger than the bottom current. That top current runs two to three knots an hour, and when you get offshore it gets even rougher, but the bottom current isn't affected. I knew this because we fished with bottom nets when shark fishing years before.

I said that was my observation all up and down the west coast, and Alaska too, with the Japanese Current. I told him all about it. But these academics, they didn't listen to me. The academics didn't value my experience. They didn't value the opinion of anyone who wasn't a scientist.

But they had a little boat, built like a submarine, called the *Alvin*. There was a shell in it so that people could go down and do underwater studies. They went offshore in it, beyond the Continental Shelf, where they found cauldrons spewing out hot water and chemicals, like undersea volcanoes. There was plant growth on the rims of the cauldrons.

They thought the upwelling of hot water came from the cauldrons and was carried down the coast by the Japanese Current, making the shallow water warmer. There were dead spots. We found a long time ago that once in a while something killed small crabs in shallow water as they shed their shells. Dead hake littered the beaches from the Alsea River to Yachats. Once we saw eight miles of dead hake. After they found the cauldrons, one of the assistants said they were the reason for the dead fish, because there's less oxygen in hot water. That made sense. He convinced me on that one.

National Fisherman *cover, December 2005*

15. Celebrations

I was one of three fellows from the west coast who won *National Fisherman* magazine's Highliner Award in 2005. I think my daughter Margaret might have had something to do with it. The three fellows they chose were from different fisheries. Besides me there was Bill Maahs, a salmon troller from California, and Bill Webber, Sr., a salmon seiner from Alaska. They had a dinner for us in Seattle in November.

After we got back to Newport, there was another dinner for me at the Oregon Coast Aquarium, in January 2006. The Port of Newport presented me with another plaque. I really enjoyed it.

Later on I went down to Palm Springs, a big tourist town, to a crowded farmer's market where they bring all their vegetables and crafts out onto the street. They close down the street for the market. It was a wide street, with a divider of palm trees in between the lanes. You have to stay with your group and not get separated, and remember where you parked your car!

I turned around and there was Bill Webber, another of the fellows who won the Highliner Award when I did. Amazing in such a crowd! I met him later on in Seattle at Fish Expo, and we had coffee down at the waterfront. Most of the guys my age have passed on in the last few years.

I've had some big birthday parties too. My 80th birthday party was in August 1999, just a few months after Joyce died. She had planned the party, and we went ahead and had it. They had another big party for me on my 85th, in 2004, and a smaller party on my 90th, combined with a Whisler family reunion.

At my 80th birthday party, 1999

On my 85th birthday, 2004

Accepting plaque for National Fisherman
Highliner Award from Port of Newport, January 2006

16. Reflections

Losing boats

In 2001 we bought the *Nordic Viking* at auction. Bill Jacobson and I bought it through the Atlantico Corporation. It was a good buy and the right time to do it because we got the crab quotas. The boat fished king crab and opilio. The former owners had been very good so the boat had a good history for getting quota.

We hired a skipper named Bill Prout to run it, and eventually sold part of the boat to him. Then we hired another skipper, for the salmon tendering season, and he ran it on the rocks. That was in July 2007. It was declared a total loss, so we sold it to the insurance company.

I haven't become particularly philosophical about losing boats. We lost the *Mary Frances*, the *Baron*, the *All Alaskan*, as well as the *Nordic Viking*, but we never lost any lives. That's remarkable when you've fished as long as I have.

Even if you lose boats, you don't give up. A lot of it is how the boat is built, so the backbone of the boat doesn't break down. The workmanship of the hull is important, and good machinery is another safety feature. You get the best engine and treat it right – change the oil and so forth. I never had a boat that I missed a season because I wasn't ready.

The Nordic Viking

Quitting fishing

By 1978, it was time to retire and be home more. I had competent skippers so it was easy to step aside. I still made arrangements at the shipyard for boats to be maintained or converted to trawl boats, but I no longer went to sea.

Even though I felt a certain peace at sea, I don't miss going to sea. I'm getting older and it's a young man's game. The older you get, you get bunged up and you can't compete. You can be on a boat longer as a skipper after serving on deck, but you have limitations.

I'm not sentimental about the years I went to sea, but I thought it was a good thing. When you are skipper, you are in command – you are at the top. You make the choices where you are going to lay the pots or drag. You make choices about the weather: will you go out or will you come in, or cross the bar? You are always making choices about safety.

Our family used to joke, "There is the Right way, the Wrong way and Hall way." The "Hall way" is usually the practical way, I guess.

It was better than working for somebody else at a steady job that never changed. It gives you a lot more knowledge about things than working at a job in one position all your life.

The moon has an awful lot to do with the tides and the tides

Even crewmen adopted the family joke. Left to right: Robbie Hall (son of John Hall, no relation), Tom Capri and Dave Wilson aboard the Provider, *1990*

have an awful lot to do with how fish migrate, inshore and offshore, depending on the time of year. I liked figuring all that out, and learning what man can overcome.

Being away from home was the worst part. It's not like a job where you come home every night. I didn't like bad weather either, when a storm was on and you couldn't get over the bar and get home because the swells were breaking and dangerous, and you couldn't fish, either.

My siblings today

My brother Raymond lives here in Newport. He was married to a woman named Annabelle. She died about ten years ago, so he is a widower now. Before she died, Annabelle asked that he take care of her best friend, Doris. Doris has heart problems so he takes her to her doctor appointments, brings food in for her, and drives her out for lunch when the weather is right. They enjoy being together.

Chester died in 2000 on my birthday. He was 82 years old. He smoked, but he didn't die from smoking. He had diabetes and Crohn's disease.

Frances died of lung cancer in 2005. She smoked too.

Mary lives in Fairbanks, Alaska. She's more than six years younger than I am, still in her eighties. She just got her undergraduate degree and goes to dances. It keeps her young.

At a family reunion in Newport, 1967. Left to right: My father, me, Frances, Raymond, Mary and Chester

With my siblings in Fairbanks, Alaska in 1997
Left to right: Mary, Frances, me, Raymond and Chester

Our dad died in 1971 at the age of 85. He spent the last fifteen years of his life in Crescent City, California, where he cut grape stakes from redwood trees to be used in vineyards. He had heart problems. My old friend Arleon Parsons had married my cousin Florence Whisler, Uncle Everett's daughter, and they lived in Crescent City too. Dad called Florence one day and said, "I don't feel well." Arleon went straight over the next day after he got back from fishing and found Dad collapsed on the floor – he'd had a stroke. He died soon afterward from pneumonia.

The meaning of life

I don't have too many more years here, but I believe that Jesus Christ is the Son of God and that the prophets forecast fulfillment.

I think the main thing in life is to find out whether or not you believe in the Savior, and if you do, follow the Christian faith as taught in the Bible. I think I've done that, but there are exceptions. That's why you need the Savior, to take care of your sins. I'm not perfect. No one is perfect, not even Christians.

I don't know what you'd call successful. If your family remains together – if you aren't divorced – I think you have a certain amount of success in life, if you maintain your faith. The Bible tells us to be "equally yoked," in other words, to have the same faith.

I don't know how I envision the future of my family company. I've read books about huge corporations that started out small, like the railroad and gasoline corporations. Then you go back east and see the homes of these corporate barons. They're mansions that have been turned into museums. I don't want that to happen in my family.

Money is only a means of exchange of things that you value. If you overspend and borrow more than you can pay back, you're in trouble. Being conservative is better. I've been conservative, I'd say, not liberal.

My advice to young people today is to get an education, but also to get experience in the real world. Take Bill Jacobson. He went to college for a while, but he says he made more money by getting out in the world, getting a job, and working up.

Sea farmer

It is hard to learn the fishing industry without participating in it. That's why I don't trust academics. You can go into it right out of school but it helps if you study fisheries. If you take something else in college it's harder.

You are in competition with other fellows when you fish. If you just want to make ends meet, you might as well be onshore. You can't catch fish by only talking about it; you have to do it.

Old Charlie Mark, a fellow that ran a fish plant in Winchester Bay, had a saying. When guys complained that they missed out on fishing back in the day, he said, "You can't catch them onshore or on the dock."

You work to catch the fish but you have to conserve it for the next year, so you should be watchful of not catching the small ones. Wait until they grow and get mature before you harvest them. Release the small ones so they can spawn. When you fish, you are a sea farmer. You have to have seed for the next season, just like a farmer. You are harvesting a crop from the sea.

Me at 94 with Kathleen

Me on a camel approaching the pyramids in Egypt, 1971

Afterword

Often I have heard the words, "I've always admired your dad," because of his remarkable personal qualities of great vision, faith, integrity and hard work. I trust these qualities come through as you read his words captured and shaped lovingly here by Teru Lundsten, in this memoir about his life as a fisherman. She, along with my sister Bonnie, felt it also important to describe his upbringing and its influences on the man he became.

The reader who knows him personally will note the absence of other facets of his life – this small volume can't possibly cover everything. Let me briefly describe a few of those here.

Dad is an innovator and vision-builder, not just in business but also in daily life. He went on annual deer hunting trips with a group of church friends. The need to transport a deer carcass over rough terrain inspired him to design and craft a carrier for the deer carcass using bicycle wheels and welded steel pipes. It was a marvelous, practical invention.

He wants to see others succeed. Over the years he supported promising fishermen he saw as hardworking and smart. He advanced them as captains, partners or even loaned money to them so that they, too, could become boat owners.

But his interest in business extends beyond fishing. With diverse partners over the years he held ownership in a grocery store, a bowling alley, various tracts of land around Newport, even a bank (where he especially enjoyed evaluating loan requests) and other ventures. A particularly dear success has been San-I-Pak Pacific, a company that manufactures waste sterilizing compactors for sale to a global market, led by partner John Hall.

My brother Vern got Dad interested in mining ores. Vern is a really good fisherman himself and invaluable to the family fishing business, but he also has a passion for geology. He developed an interest in gold mining and formed a partnership for us to mine gold in the Yukon. Dad went on to invest in various mining companies and tracks their prices closely on a tablet he keeps near his chair in the living room.

"Determination" could have been Dad's middle name. There are many examples that could illustrate this, though one stands out. When his efforts to build a fish plant and boat yard fell through on Yaquina Bay, he set sights on mining limestone in Idaho. In his seventies, he bought claims, re-opened a quarry and built a milling plant to fulfill a vision he had. The family is finally developing the Yaquina Bay property into an industrial park.

On the other hand, Dad wasn't all work and no play. He particularly enjoys visiting friends and family members, and has traveled great distances to do so. We took a family car trip nearly every year to California to visit Mom's relatives. In 1953 we toured the United States to visit Dad's sister Frances in Birmingham, Alabama, taking the southern route, then on around to Washington, D.C., New York, the Great Lakes area and Montana. In 1956 we pulled a trailer house to Fairbanks, Alaska to visit Dad's sister Mary. He sang and sometimes yodeled while he drove to entertain us kids on those long drives.

Dad, Mom and I toured Europe in 1969 to see the lands of early Christianity and visit Bonnie in Germany. Later Dad sailed with son-in-law Peter (my sister Janet's husband) on a guided missile cruiser from Honolulu to San Diego. He loved that experience! On another trip, my parents visited Janet and Peter in Singapore. As our extended family grew to include grandchildren, we met for business meetings in Hawaii, Mexico and Venezuela. Family connections continue to be an important value to Dad.

The most important factor in my dad's life is his religious beliefs. He is a devoted Christian, a Gideon member, and served as Sunday school teacher, Deacon and Elder at Newport First Christian Church. He always tried to be a role model for us children, as his grandfather was for him. His stories were often a lesson with a moral tale based on scripture. Without a doubt, he would say his life purpose is to go to heaven, not to be the successful fisherman he was known to be.

However, my dad's life would not have been the same without the supporting role of our mother, Dorothy Joyce Curryer. She deserves kudos as she contributed so much to his success.

Our parents married soon after her high school graduation and Mom became the anchor of our home life. With three children (excluding me – I came later) and a husband who was on the water much of the time, she packed them up and traveled up or down the coast to be at the port of delivery for a few days. Sometimes she spent a month in Eureka when that was the port of convenience. Mom soon learned to be self-reliant and independent, and so enjoyed being a mother. She took Home Extension courses to improve her homemaking knowledge. She sewed our dresses, she canned tuna, she baked pies, she knit sweaters. She also drove us to cheerleading practices, church camps, 4-H camps and music lessons. We children were the focus of her attention. Later, when I was the only one home, Mom became a nurse's aide not for the money but for the opportunity to care for others, especially the babies.

Mom also brought music into our home. She sang in the church choir, taught herself to play the piano, and danced to American Bandstand on Saturday mornings. She ensured that each of her children had some sort of musical training. In her honor, a scholarship (administered by Bonnie) is given each year to a Newport High School graduate to pursue his or her musical talents.

The other great joy of hers was community service. Her leadership skills eventually evolved into her participation on the first Oregon Coast Aquarium board, the pinnacle of her volunteerism.

As much as my brother, sisters and I miss our mother, we are glad that Dad found companionship with his second wife, Kathleen. Her sweet sense of humor and sunny disposition are dear assets to both him and us.

The gifts my siblings and I received from our parents are many. Besides the security of a stable home, the most obvious one is opportunity. Both Mom and Dad encouraged us to fulfill our aspirations. Perhaps because Dad's mother was a teacher and education was something she treasured, he wanted to pass on her passion for learning as well as ensure we had the skills to support ourselves.

In closing, I want to thank my sister Bonnie for her support and for encouraging Dad and me in this endeavor, as well as Teru for her professional help and patience.

Margaret Hall
October 20, 2014

Chronology

1919 – August 9. Born in American Falls, Idaho

1921 – Family moved near Kendrick, Idaho

1922 – Family moved near Moscow, Idaho

1923 – Family moved near Kuna, Idaho then into Meridian, Idaho

1924 – Family moved to Vernonia, Oregon

1926 – Lived with Uncle Bill in Boise, Idaho

1927 – Returned to Vernonia, Oregon

1930 – Moved with father and brothers to Waldport, Oregon

1934 – Mother died

1937 – Graduated from high school
       Purchased the *Sea Falcon*, nicknamed the *Tupper*, with brothers

1940 – Built the *Mary Frances* with brothers

1941 – June 15. Married Dorothy Joyce Curryer
       Newlyweds moved to Nye Beach in Newport, Oregon

1942 – Daughter Bonnie born
       Family moved to house on Abbey Street in Newport

1943 – Lost the *Mary Frances*
       Brothers built the *Ruth Ellen* and purchased the *Sunset*

1944 – Daughter Janet born
       Brothers built the *Christian*

1945 – Son Vern born

1948 – Brothers dissolved partnership

1949 – Sold the *Christian*
    Purchased the *Sea Breeze II*
    Daughter Margaret born

1960 – Saw Unidentified Flying Object at sea

1961 – Art Paris took the *Sea Breeze II* to Alaska
    to test the Dungeness crab fishery as a distant water fishery

1962 – Purchased the *King and Winge*
    Left Dungeness crab fishery

1963 – Took the *King and Winge* to Alaska to fish king crab
    (first time I fished there)

1966 – Purchased the *Rondys*
    December 6. Severed my left hand

1968 – Formed Rondys, Inc. in Oregon

1969 – Lobbied Congress to help make federal loans available to commercial fishermen

1971 – Father died
    Sold *Sea Breeze II*

1972 – Built the *Provider*
    Formed King and Winge, Inc. in Washington
    Formed Rondys, Inc. in Washington

1973 – Purchased the *Atlantico* and the *Baron*
    Lost the *Baron*

1975 – Built the *Progress*
    Rondys and *Progress* entered the bairdi crab fishery

1976 – Formed All Alaskan Seafoods, Inc. (AAS) with other Kodiak fishermen to operate processor-at-sea

1978 – Last year actively fished, on the *Progress*
    Served on Oregon Sea Grant Advisory Board until 1985

1982 – Purchased the *Vanguard* (already part-owned by son Vern)
       Entered pollock and opilio fisheries
       AAS bought Star of Kodiak processing plant in Kodiak, Alaska

1985 – Purchased the *Argosy* and the *Alsea*
       Hired daughter Margaret

1986 – Purchased the *Sourdough*
       Lost the *All Alaskan* (replaced 1995)

1994 – AAS formed joint venture with Russians
       Sold Star of Kodiak to Trident Seafoods

1995 – Sent *Rondys* and *Sourdough* to crab in Sea of Okhotsk
       (for Russian joint venture)
       AAS bought and converted *Rybak Chokotki* as mother ship
       (venture completed 2001)

1999 – May 4. Wife Joyce died

2000 – July 22. Married Kathleen Weber

2001 – Purchased *Nordic Viking*

2005 – November 18. Received *National Fisherman* magazine
       Highliner Award

2007 – Lost *Nordic Viking*

2012 – Diagnosed with Parkinson's disease

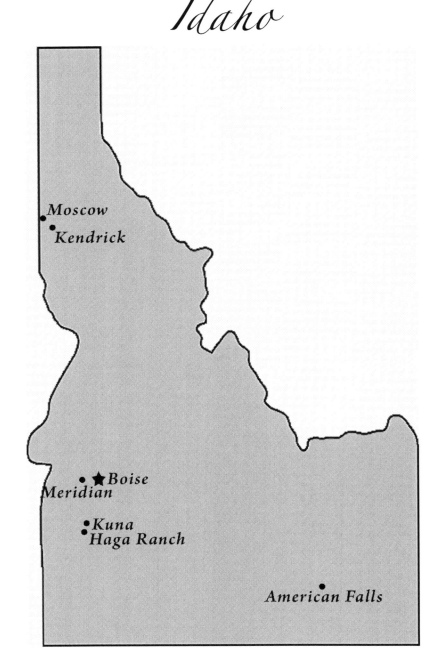

Where I've lived in
Oregon

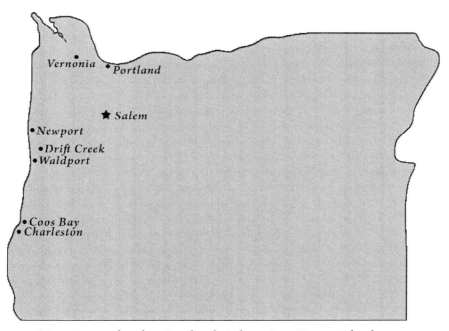

Note: I never lived in Portland, Salem, Coos Bay or Charleston - reference points only

Family

Grandparents
Paternal grandfather: Wilburn Hall (1857-1945)
Paternal grandmother: Elizabeth Frasure Hall (1856-1933)
Maternal grandfather: John Bernice Whisler (1846-1936)
Maternal grandmother: Sarah Elizabeth Denney Whisler (1855-1890)

Parents
Father: Evan Silas Hall (1885-1971)
Mother: Ruth Ellen Whisler Hall (1886-1934)
    Married 1916

Siblings
Chester Lee Hall (1917-2000)
John Raymond Hall (Born 1917)
    Twins
Frances Hall Leaver (1922 – 2005)
Mary Hall Binkley (Born 1926)

Wives
Dorothy Joyce Curryer Hall (1925-1999)
    Married 1941, mother of four children
Kathleen Weber Hall (Born 1929)
    Married 2000

Children
Bonnie Hall Elerding (Born 1942)
Janet Hall Long (Born 1944)
Vern Hall (Born 1945)
Margaret Hall (Born 1949)

Eight grandchildren (one deceased)

Five great-grandchildren

Made in the USA
Las Vegas, NV
01 August 2021